HOW TO HAVE GREAT SEX

A COMPLETE GUIDE ON MAKING LOVE AND MIND-BLOWING SEX

AVENTURAS DE VIAJE

Illustrated by
NEIL GERMIO

Copyright SF Nonfiction Books © 2013

www.SFNonfictionBooks.com

All Rights Reserved
No part of this document may be reproduced without written consent from the author.

WARNINGS AND DISCLAIMERS

The information in this publication is made public for reference only.

Neither the author, publisher, nor anyone else involved in the production of this publication is responsible for how the reader uses the information or the result of his/her actions.

CONTENTS

Introduction   xiii

THE BASICS OF GREAT SEX

Overcoming Roadblocks   3

FOREPLAY

Basic Escalation   9
Bathing Together   10
Food Play   11
Games   13
Porn   14
Sexy Talk   15
Touch   17
Kissing   20
Massage   23
Getting Undressed   30
Oral Sex   33

Intercourse   39
Getting 'Freaky'   43

YOGA FOR BETTER SEX

Introduction   51
Chakras   53
Full-Stomach Breathing   54
Solo Yoga Routine   55
Partnered Yoga Routine   78
Quick Lists   89

126 SEX POSITIONS GUARANTEED TO SPICE UP YOUR BEDROOM

Introduction	93

MAN ON TOP

Position 1. 1st Posture	97
Position 2. 2nd Posture	98
Position 3. 3rd Posture	99
Position 4. 4th Posture	100
Position 5. Bridal Bridge	101
Position 6. Backward Bending Flower	102
Position 7. 7th Posture	103
Position 8. 8th Posture	104
Position 9. Ape	105
Position 10. 10th Posture	106
Position 11. 11th Posture	107
Position 12. Level-Feet	108
Position 13. Pine Tree	109
Position 14. Rising Star	110
Position 15. Splitting	111
Position 16. Tail of the Ostrich	113
Position 17. Swallows In Love	114
Position 18. Yawning	115
Position 19. Dragon Turns Away	117
Position 20. G-Spot Stimulator	118
Position 21. Crab	119
Position 22. Dragon Turn	120
Position 23. Galloping Horse	121
Position 24. Gaping	122
Position 25. Gripping With Toes	123
Position 26. Huge Bird Above a Red Sea	124
Position 27. One Who Stops at Home	125
Position 28. Placid Embrace	126
Position 29. Pressing	127
Position 30. Raised Feet	128
Position 31. Refined Position	129
Position 32. Silkworm Spinning a Cocoon	130
Position 33. Stopperage	131

Position 34. Twining	132
Position 35. Clasping	133
Position 36. Fixing a Nail	134
Position 37. Half Pressed	136
Position 38. Horse Shakes Feet	138
Position 39. Splitting Of Bamboo	139
Position 40. Ankle Hold	140
Position 41. Fetal Flower	141
Position 42. Encircling	142
Position 43. Held Feet	143
Position 44. Horse Cross Feet	144
Position 45. Intact Posture	145
Position 46. Jade Joint	146
Position 47. Joining the Lotus	147
Position 48. Lotus	148
Position 49. Mandarin Duck	149
Position 50. Phoenix Playing in a Red Cave	150
Position 51. Pressed	151
Position 52. Pumping the Well	152
Position 53. Turning	153
Position 54. Rising	154
Position 55. Turtle Move	155
Position 56. Wife of Indra	156

WOMAN ON TOP

Position 57. Butterflies in Flight	159
Position 58. Fish	160
Position 59. Interchange of Coition	161
Position 60. Inverted Embrace	162
Position 61. Sharing Reins	163
Position 62. Accomplishing Position	164
Position 63. Alternative Movement of Piercing	165
Position 64. Frog Fashion	166
Position 65. Kama's Wheel	167
Position 66. Crying Out	169
Position 67. Lotus Inverted	170
Position 68. Loving Lift	171
Position 69. Paired Feet	172
Position 70. Position of Equals	173
Position 71. Singing Monkey	174

Position 72. Snake Trap	175
Position 73. Yin and Yang	176
Position 74. Ascending Position	177
Position 75. Butterfly	178
Position 76. Cat and Mouse Sharing a Hole	179
Position 77. Catbird Seat	180
Position 78. Love Seat	181
Position 79. Orgasmic Role-Reversal	182
Position 80. Pair of Tongs	183
Position 81. Race of the Member	184
Position 82. Hanging Bow	185
Position 83. Spider	186
Position 84. Goat and the Tree	187
Position 85. Mare	188
Position 86. Rabbit Grooming	189
Position 87. Reciprocal Sights of the Posteriors	190
Position 88. Reverse Crab	191
Position 89. Swing	192
Position 90. Spinning the Top	193
Position 91. Topping and Turning	195

FROM BEHIND

Position 92. 6th Posture (Doggy Style)	199
Position 93. Loving Chair	200
Position 94. Rising Pillows	201
Position 95. Standing Doggy	202
Position 96. Tiger Step	203
Position 97. White Tiger	204
Position 98. Cicada on a Bough	205
Position 99. Coitus from Behind	206
Position 100. Elephant	207
Position 101. Congress of a Cow	208
Position 102. The 'Quickie'	209
Position 103. Freestanding Love	210
Position 104. Late Spring Donkey	211
Position 105. 9th Posture	212
Position 106. Loving Gaze	213
Position 107. Standing Spontaneity	214

STANDING POSITIONS

Position 108. Bamboo	217
Position 109. Belly to Belly	218
Position 110. Driving the Peg Home	219
Position 111. Standing Split	220
Position 112. Supported Congress	221
Position 113. Suspended Congress	222
Position 114. Weeping Willow	223
Position 115. Wheelbarrow	224

SIDE ON POSITIONS

Position 116. Transverse Lute	227
Position 117. Cicada to the Side	228
Position 118. Mandarin Ducks	229
Position 119. Two Fishes	230
Position 120. 5th Posture	231

MISCELLANEOUS POSITIONS

Position 121. Autumn Dog	235
Position 122. Fitter-In	236
Position 123. Drawing the Bow	237
Position 124. Scissors	238
Position 125. Sitting on Top of the World	239
Position 126. Seagulls on the Wing	240

BONUS - ORAL POSITIONS

All For Her	243
Lean Back	244
Riding His Face	245
Sideways 69	246
69 Her On Top	247
69 Him on Top	248
Standing 69	249

LEARN TANTRIC SEX

Understanding Tantric Sex	253
The Mindset of an Amazing Sexual Being	255
Your Tantric Space	256

Chakras	257
Namaste Ritual	258
Tantric Taste Test	259
Breathing	261
Understanding and Improving Orgasm	265
Self-Exploration	269
Masturbation	273
Redirecting Sexual Energy	278
Peaking	280
Tantric Massage	282
Tantric Dancing	284
Tantric Oral	286
Sexual Poses for Tantric Sex	287
After Climax	289
30 More Tantric Meditations and Exercises	290
References	303
Author Recommendations	305
About Aventuras	307

THANKS FOR YOUR PURCHASE

Did you know you can get FREE chapters of any SF Nonfiction Book you want?

https://offers.SFNonfictionBooks.com/Free-Chapters

You will also be among the first to know of FREE review copies, discount offers, bonus content, and more.

Go to:

https://offers.SFNonfictionBooks.com/Free-Chapters

Thanks again for your support.

INTRODUCTION

Despite the title, this book is about much more than having great sex. It is about having the most fantastic, amazing, mind-blowing, incredible sex you have ever had.

By reading and practicing what is inside this book, you will learn about yourself and your lover in the most intimate way. If that is too deep for you, then just have fun exploring your and your lover's bodies.

If you currently have a lover, you are encouraged to read this book together. If you do not currently have a lover, you can still gain a lot. You will improve yourself and your sexual knowledge, which will also enhance your attractiveness to potential partners.

The material for this book has been taken from a variety of schools of thought (Kama Sutra, Ananga Ranga, The Perfumed Garden, Taoist sexual practices, tantric sex, etc.) and compiled in a way to give you all the information you need to experience the best sex you've ever had.

Amazing sex means different things to different people. This book encompasses many different ideas. What you try is up to you, but you will benefit most if you venture beyond your comfort zone. It may be the best experience you've ever known, but if you never try, you'll never know.

This publication is presented in four parts.

1. The Basics of Great Sex

If you only read one part of this book, make it this one. It takes you from foreplay to intercourse to "taboo" practices.

2. Yoga for Better Sex

This section contains solo and partnered yoga routines specifically designed to increase your sexual pleasure and create a deeper connection between you and your lover.

3. 126 Sex Positions

This part of the book presents a complete range of poses, combining all the famous books including Kama Sutra, Ananga Ranga, The Perfumed Garden, and more.

4. Learn Tantric Sex

This section explains everything you need to know about tantric sex. Learn what it is and how you can use it to increase sexual pleasure, have sexual awakenings, and connect with yourself and your lover on a deeper level.

THE BASICS OF GREAT SEX

OVERCOMING ROADBLOCKS

Take Care of Yourself

If you don't feel good about yourself, how can you expect to make your partner feel good?

Improve yourself where you can, and don't worry about where you can't. Not only will you be more attractive to the opposite sex, you will feel more sexual.

Be clean, smell nice, get a haircut (in all areas; you can trim each other), clean your nails, look after your teeth and breath (brush, floss, and use mouthwash), eat right, exercise regularly, etc.

Dress and accessorize the way you want (if you want).

Piercings in certain places, such as the nipples, navel, labia, and tongue, can be highly erotic.

Don't worry about your physical aspects that you can't change, such as the size of your penis or breasts. They are beautiful, erotic, and desirable the way they are.

Communication

Be open with each other about what you do and do not enjoy, as well as things that you may wish to experiment with (this book offers plenty of ideas).

Be aware of non-verbal communication. For example, your lover's breathing can give you insight into their emotional state. It may be steady and calm, erratic and stressed, deep and aroused, etc.

Age

Getting older should not keep you from having amazing sex. The fact that you're older means you have more experience and are more in tune with your body. Stay attractive to yourself and your lover(s) by keeping up to date with the current style for your age. Accept your body as it is now, and use plenty of lubrication.

Erectile Dysfunction

An occasional letdown is normal and should be ignored, especially if it is your first time having sex with a new lover or you are an older man. Don't make a big deal out of it. Placing the flaccid penis inside the vagina may be enough to stimulate the erection. If that doesn't work, you can still pleasure your lover with your mouth, hands, or toys.

If you're under forty-five, your issue is probably mental. You need to enhance your confidence. Staying away from drugs and alcohol (including tobacco) will also help. Drugs like Viagra or herbal remedies like ginseng, as well as cock rings, may help, but should only be used as directed.

During lengthy love-making, it is normal for erections to come and go. When this happens, just increase manual and/or oral stimulation.

Lasting Longer With Peaking

Peaking is an exercise that can be done during intercourse or masturbation. It is an effective way for men to last longer. It can also be used by either sex to build up sexual energy, which will increase sexual pleasure. It is done by starting and stopping stimulation at various stages of arousal.

First find your point of no return. Give the stages of your arousal a scale from zero to 10. Zero is no arousal and ten is orgasm. Nine is your point of no return—that is, the point where it wouldn't matter if you stopped stimulation; you would still climax. You want to get to a 7 or 8 and stay there until you choose to climax.

Once you reach level 8, stop stimulation and re-direct your focus. Once your arousal has gone down to a 5 or 6, restart stimulation. Do this a few times before allowing yourself to climax. Other patterns you can use are:

- Peak, plateau, peak higher, plateau etc.
- Peak, plateau, decrease, peak a little higher than before, decrease, peak a little higher still, etc.

You can also try any other patterns you can think of until you discover what will work to control your arousal level without having to stop completely. Make a goal to last 30 minutes without stopping.

If needed, you can use peaking during intercourse by taking your penis out and changing positions, massaging, switching to oral stimulation, etc., until your arousal goes down.

Blocking the Flow

Below are some ways men can block the release of fluid during ejaculation.

Note: Some people consider blocking the flow to be unnatural and harmful.

- Press very hard with your finger on the point halfway along the perineum.
- Grasp the head of your penis around the coronal ridge with your finger and thumb, and squeeze hard.
- Pull down firmly on your scrotum.
- Squeeze your pubococcygeus muscle (PC) muscle tightly and take a deep, sharp breath.

Pregnancy

Heightened sensitivity in the breasts, as well as nausea and vomiting in the first trimester, may affect your sex life during pregnancy, but it is physically impossible for a man's penis to come into contact with the fetus.

Use woman-on-top or rear-entry positions. Lie on top of your partner, with your legs either between his or outside them. Straddling him, lying on your side, or lying on your back with him coming in from the side are also good positions. If your back aches, then try classic doggy style.

If She Can't Orgasm

When a woman cannot orgasm, it is usually due to psychological barriers. Train yourself using masturbation.

Get yourself relaxed and be sure you won't be interrupted. Start with a bath and self-exploration. Once you move to your genitals, imagine you are the type of woman who loves sex and who has orgasms easily. Move your hips like a sexy woman. Don't focus on having an orgasm. Just let it come. Use a dildo or other toys if you need to. Once you can bring yourself to orgasm, try with a lover.

For a detailed description of self-exploration, see the Self-Exploration chapter in the Learn Tantric Sex section.

Related Chapters:

- Self-Exploration
- Masturbation

FOREPLAY

Foreplay is everything that leads up to sex, including sexual tension and romance.

It can begin hours, days or even weeks before the act. In fact, it never has to stop.

The key to great foreplay, as to great sex, is to focus on your partner's pleasure. And when he/she is focusing on your pleasure, experience it with all your senses.

BASIC ESCALATION

Women (usually) take a lot longer to reach a state of arousal ready for intercourse than men do. If the woman is given the time to reach this state then she will receive greater pleasure during sex. What follows is an example of escalating slowly to allow this state of arousal to be achieved.

1. Hug and caress.
2. Play with her hair and tell her how much you like her scent (or perfume or smell).
3. Kiss, first lightly and then passionately.
4. As you undress, spend a long time cuddling and stroking and hugging close.
5. Towards the end of the all-over body pleasure, caress her genitals.
6. Do not go for intercourse until she is extremely aroused.

When You're Not Around

Just because you're not physically there with each other does not mean you can't engage in amazing foreplay. Phone sex, sexy messages (text, email etc.) and love notes are great for building anticipation. Call your lover at work to say something sexy, slip a note and/or a sexy picture into their lunch, etc.

Romantic gestures are also great. Send flowers to your lover at work, lay rose petals from the front door to the bedroom, and greet them with a glass of wine. Doing nice things for each other in general shows you care and is an underrated turn-on.

Related Chapters:

- Intercourse

BATHING TOGETHER

Bathing together can be a very sensual way to connect with your lover before, during, and after sex, especially if you've been playing with sticky and/or tasty substances.

You can set the mood with bubbles, candles, and music. When you're bathing your lover, let them know that they need not lift a finger. You may want to tie them to the shower head. Pay attention to every inch of your lover's body, using your hands to give them a slippery massage. Linger on certain spots, beginning with nonsexual areas. Give your lover a head massage as you wash their hair, and don't forget to wash the perineum and anal passage. Be careful when washing the genitals—under the foreskin, for example—as soap can sting.

If this leads to sex, be careful on slippery surfaces. If your tub is small, sit up together.

After the bath or shower slowly dry your lover from their face down to their toes with a soft towel, following with soft kisses. If you want, rub your lover down with moisturizer.

Related Chapters:

- Massage

FOOD PLAY

Serve and share food in a seductive way. Laugh, talk, and flirt while eating with your lover. Serve fresh foods and include a variety of flavors and scents. Choose foods with pleasing smells, suggestive shapes (e.g., cucumbers), bright colors, and a variety of textures. Don't rush your meals; allow yourselves time to savor the smell and taste of each bite.

Note: You may need to lay down some towels or plastic sheeting for some of these activities, as they can get messy.

- Arrange your favorite flavors/foods, such as chocolate, honey, whipped cream, champagne, or fruits, on your lover, then lick your lover clean.
- Put some warm honey in a plastic bag. Cut a small hole in the corner and stream it steadily over your lover's genitals. Afterwards, lick it off.
- Feed your lover their favorite ice cream. Spill a bit in places of choice. Clean it up with your tongue.
- Fill the bathtub up with champagne and take a bath together.
- While dining, use your feet under the table to bring your lover to orgasm.
- Give your server a sexy note to give to your partner during the evening.
- Blindfold your lover and feed them a variety of tasty tidbits.
- Have a naked food fight, and then clean up with your mouths.
- Include a sexy note and/or picture in your lover's lunch or send it with chocolates to their workplace. You could include a banana with suggestions on how they could enjoy it.
- Fill water pistols with wine and have a "water fight," then lick each other clean.

- Put a small amount of honey somewhere on your body which your lover needs to find with their tongue.
- Feed her using your penis as a spoon, while she uses her naked body as plate.

GAMES

Sexual games are only limited by your imagination. Most drinking or betting games can be used, and if you need more ideas, the internet is filled with them. Here are a few to get you started.

- Leave a trail of clues (underwear, flower petals, etc.) for your lover leading to your love nest (where ever you want them to find you).
- First person to roll a six is the boss for the night.
- Bet on anything. The loser owes the winner a sexual favor of the winner's choice.
- Get two dice. Each number on the first die represents a body part, such as the chest, mouth, genitals, or ears, while the numbers of the other die represent an action (suck, lick, massage, etc.). Take turns rolling and doing what the dice command.
- Using watercolor paints, paint each other.
- Have three lists: sexual acts/positions, places, and times. Pick one from each list and do it.
- Spell out things you can do to your lover on their back with your tongue. If they guess it, you do it.
- Truth or dare, adult version.
- Twister, naked.
- Write anything you want to do with your partner, whether sexual or not, on strips of paper. These could be positions, places, or date nights. Pull the activities out of a hat and do them.
- Oil up and have a wrestling match. A protective ground sheet is suggested.

PORN

Porn can be a great stimulator as well as a learning tool, but be aware that a lot of it is made for visual stimulation and my not feel good to your lover. You can watch porn together for ideas and/or act out what the actors do. If you don't like pornographic movies, then erotic photo magazines and/or stories may be more your thing.

The act of making porn (movies, pictures, or erotica) can be a great turn-on for some. If you do want to make your own, it is important that you agree on what will come of the finished product—whether you will erase it, take it to swingers, or hide it, for example. You may also want to discuss what poses or positions you want to use. You could re-enact a movie scene or make up your own.

Using the same room you would normally have sex in is a good place to start. After you are more comfortable, you can use other locations. You may need to adjust the lighting so the picture is not too dark for the camera. Test different sources (sunlight, dimmed lights, candles, etc.) to see what you prefer.

If you're making a movie, use a wide shot. You can hook the camera to the TV so you can see (and adjust) as you film. Watch the playback of the two of you on camera for foreplay or during sex. If you want to watch but don't want to tape it, set up one or more mirrors.

If you take still pictures, you can send them to each other in all sorts of ways. One idea for erotic writing is to write exactly what you want to do to your lover and send it off to them, with or without a sexy picture of yourself.

SEXY TALK

Sexy or "dirty" talk can be great to turn your lover on over the phone, just before intercourse. or during the act.

How explicit your sexy talk gets is up to you. For some, natural (or enhanced) moans and grunts are enough. Telling your lover how good they look, expressing your feelings (without going in to a deep conversation) or reciting poetry while making love may also do the trick.

For those who want a little more, such talk usually means describing what you and your lover are doing, are going to do, or want to do/have done.

Some like explicit or aggressive language, and others like romantic nothings whispered to them. Whatever the case, know what the limit is before your lover finds it offensive.

Ask what they finds a turn-on and a turn-off or an offense. This includes using different names for the genitalia.

Here are some ideas for sexy talk. Use descriptive language and details.

- Describe what you plan to do or wish you were doing to your lover.
- Describe what you wish your lover was doing to you.
- Tell the story of the first time you had sex with your lover.
- For phone sex or online chat, an easy start is "What are you wearing?" Progress from there.
- Tell your lover exactly what you are doing while you masturbate.
- Tell each other what you like, especially while your partner is doing it.

- If you need more pointers, try calling a phone sex line. If it is live, you can ask for advice. Watching/reading porn will also give you ideas. Read the material to each other.

Related Chapters:

- Porn

TOUCH

Every touch has some kind of intent. It may be playful, erotic, commanding, etc. Keep your awareness on how you touch and what it feels like to be touched. Don't think about too much; just let your body respond.

Ask your lover how the way you touch them feels, and notice their reaction. If you are the one being touched, touch your own erogenous zones at the same time.

Blindfold your naked lover and have them lay down. Touch them with a variety of different things, such as your hair, feathers, fingertips, mouth, tongue, feet, sex toys, ice cubes, fur, velvet, hands, silk, or breath. Touch in spots that usually don't get much attention, using a variety of pressures and speeds. Contrast the sensations. For example, follow a feather with an ice cube.

Spanking can be a playful way to introduce pleasure and pain, and can be incorporated into role-play, including S&M. If your partner is a man, strike him on the chest repeatedly while getting more and more "angry'"; if your partner is a woman, give her a slap on the bum followed by a gentle rub, then repeat it on the other bum cheek.

Embracing Each Other

Embracing can be done anytime in everyday life, as well as in the lead-up to sex.

Soul Embrace

Press your foreheads together and look deeply into each other's eyes. Feel each other's breath.

Caressing Embrace

She presses up against him and he caresses her breasts.

Wrapping Embrace

They stand facing each other as she wraps herself around him.

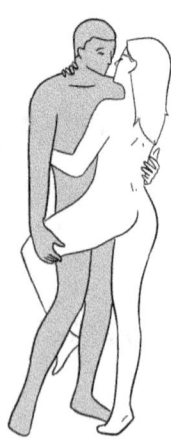

Full Embrace

She sits on his lap, as close as possible, and then wraps herself on him as he embraces her closely.

Can't Wait Embrace

He presses her up against a wall, covering her body.

KISSING

Be attentive when you kiss, for every kiss. Have soft lips and fresh breath.

Shake off the nerves and enjoy the anticipation. Get close and comfortable, make eye contact, and then bring your lips close together. Keep your lips relaxed.

Stop for second or two before actually kissing. Close your eyes if you wish, savor the feeling, and go in with closed lips.

Start soft and slowly gather momentum by opening your mouth just a little, caressing as you kiss (but don't do too much groping).

Kiss different body parts with different techniques, such as gentle biting or sucking.

Alternatively, start with other body parts before moving to the lips.

On a hot night, you and your lover can take turns licking and blowing each other's skin. When you lick your lover, try making your tongue into a point.

French Kiss

Both of you open your mouths a little more, keeping your lips gently pressed together.

Keep your tongues relaxed and gently put them in each other's mouths. Don't use too much tongue or slobber.

You can gently twirl around the tip of your lover's tongue or gently suck on it.

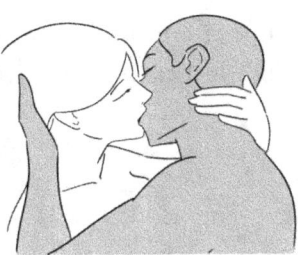

Kiss From Behind

Come from behind and softly kiss your lover until they focus all their attention on you.

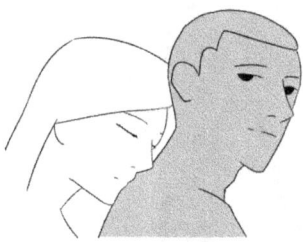

Pressing Kiss

Look your lover in the eye and pinch their lower lip with your fingers.

Caress it with your tongue, then press your lips tightly against theirs.

Splitting Kiss

One of you kisses the upper lip while the other kisses the lower. Every now and again, lightly brush your lover's lip with the tip of your tongue.

MASSAGE

Massage doesn't always have to lead to sex, but the massage techniques described in this book are meant for the progression, and are also to be used during intercourse.

Note: Don't massage your lover if he/she has recently been in, or still is, of ill health. If in doubt, seek medical advice.

Your love nest is also the perfect environment for massage. Have sensual music, soft textures, dim lights and incense. You may also want to put towels down if you are using massage oils. If you are, ensure your lover is not allergic and that anything you are using on the genitals will not burn and will be condom-compatible (if that is an issue). Sandalwood, patchouli, jasmine, and coconut oils are recommended.

Whether you are giving or receiving, do not think of the massage as leading to sex or get distracted by any worries. Focus on the pleasure and fully experience the massage. If you are the receiver, feel free to express yourself fully as you receive your massage. Make sounds and move in any way you wish. Emotional discharge is encouraged.

If you are the one giving the massage, remove all jewelry and ensure you do not have sharp nails. Put a good amount of oil in your hands and warm it by rubbing your hands together. Massage with love and confidence. Be aware of your movements and repeat them in rhythm before moving to the next stroke.

Always maintain some contact, and use your whole hand throughout the massage (not just your fingers) as well as other parts of your body, such as your hair, breasts, feet, breath, elbows, penis, or mouth, if you wish.

If you want you can ask for feedback from the receiver about how they want to be touched, where you should linger, etc. You can also just move the way you feel their body wants. Don't press on joints or bones, and gradually increase the eroticism of your massage (if you're so inclined). For an extra-erotic massage, you can get into a mutual oral position and massage each other, without touching the genitals at first.

Sample Massage

Here is a sample massage which you can use as a model, or just use the strokes to do what you wish.

Work on each area for a few minutes, gradually increasing pressure with each stroke. Re-apply oil as needed and remind your lover to breathe and relax throughout.

Start with you lover naked on their stomach. Rest your warmed and oiled hands on either side of the base of your lover's spine. Spread the oil over your lover's back using your whole hand. Move from the base up to the neck and back down the sides. Do not press on their spine directly. Repeat this while gradually increasing pressure.

Grab the large area of skin on the shoulders with both hands. Gently pull and squeeze, then release. Gradually increase pressure.

Next, press your thumbs into the back of your lover's shoulder. Your fingers should rest in the dip above the collarbone. Knead the muscle with your hands, using slow circles.

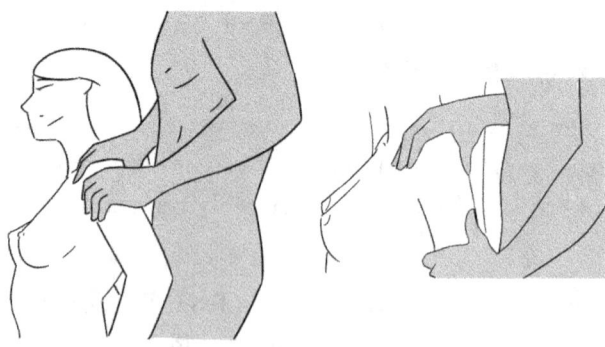

Note: These same techniques can be used while your lover is sitting, as shown in the pictures.

Go back to the long strokes you started with, rubbing all along your lover's back, then down their arms and legs to their feet.

Hold your lover's foot with your thumbs on the soles and your fingers on top. Squeeze it. Next, slide your thumbs along the bottom of their foot, and finish by squeezing each of their toes.

Use long strokes from their feet up to very close to their genitals and back down to their feet. Slide your fingers up and down in opposing directions on their calf. Next, use thumb circles, and finally use a clawing motion with your fingertips.

Use the same technique on your lover's thighs as you did on their neck. Add some light kisses to their inner thighs and some feather-light touches, like those of a spider, with your fingertips.

Place your hands on your lover's bum cheeks and lean your weight onto your hands. Press the muscles using the tips of your fingers as well as your palm heel and fists.

Finish by spreading your fingers and pressing your nails into the buttocks. Do it hard enough to leave an impression, but not too hard.

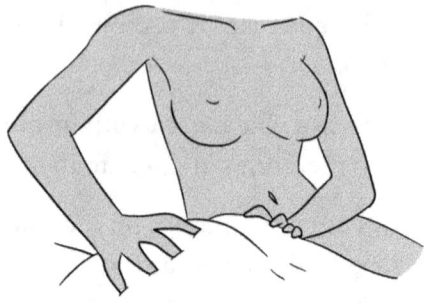

Go back to whole-body strokes, and then work your lover's arms in the same way as you did their legs. That is, use the same techniques on their hands as on their feet, on their forearms as on their calves, and on their upper arms as on their thighs.

Make small, deep movements with your thumbs and/or fingers all over their back. Finish with gentle stroking as you did at the start. Every stroke should lighter until you are using feather-light fingertip strokes, as you did on their thighs.

Ask your lover to turn onto their back.

Place your hand on the bottom of their chest, slightly angled toward the middle, with your fingers facing toward one of their shoulders.

Slowly slide your hand over their chest towards the shoulder your fingers are facing. Use no pressure. Before this stroke ends, start again with your other hand. As you pass over your lover's nipple, give it a light squeeze. After a few strokes, repeat the movement on the other side.

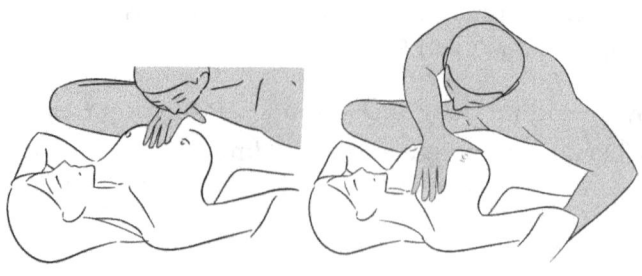

Using a very light touch with your fingertip, start on the outside of your lover's chest/breast and slowly circle around a few times. After a few circles, spiral in until you end on your lover's nipple.

Place the fingertips of both your hands on one side of your lover's chest on either side of the nipple. Slowly spread your hands apart and away from their nipple, ten bring them back up toward it

Use long strokes down the chest and belly, brushing ever closer to your lover's genitals.

Massage the front of their thighs as you did the back of them, moving up to the genitals for a gentle stroke/kiss/lick every now and then.

His Genitals

Use plenty of oil all over your lover's penis, testicles, and perineum. Use long strokes, moving up and over his penis toward his chest, out to the side, and then down over his stomach. Continue the stroke down over his penis toward you, down his legs, and then back up.

Gently hold his penis, rotate it clockwise, and slide your hands over it. Then rotate it counterclockwise.

Hold his penis in the center with both hands and pull your hands apart along his penis so one ends at the base and the other at the tip. Keep your hand on the base and press his penis against his body for a couple of seconds, then release the pressure and let your hands meet in the middle again. Repeat this a few times.

With two fingers, make small circles on his perineum. With your other hand, press on the center of his forehead with your finger.

Press his perineum and use upward strokes from the top of his nose to his hairline.

Slide your hand down his shaft. As it reaches the base, start the other hand at the top so it is a continuous stroke.

Use both hands on the shaft. Use a twisting motion, but don't grip the penis. Your hands should slide in opposite directions.

Use the continuous downward stroke again. Do it 10 times, then stop and squeeze firmly, but not too hard, for a few seconds. Do it again nine times, then eight, etc. When you reach zero, ask him to take a deep breath and tense his whole body for 15 seconds, then relax completely.

Note: If he is approaching climax during the massage, just ease off until his arousal subsides, then continue. Once the massage has been completed, if he wants, you can bring him to climax in any way the two of you wish.

Her Genitals

Rest one of your hands on your lover's vagina and the other on her heart.

Using a light touch, slowly stroke up (not in) her vagina. Let two fingers slide between her inner and outer labia as you stroke up. Circle your finger around her clitoris. Don't touch it directly.

Pull gently on her pubic hair. Pull harder if she wants.

With a slow and gentle whole-handed pinching motion, squeeze the lips of her vagina together.

With a finger from each hand, start at her perineum and stroke around the outside of the vagina on both sides, ending above her clitoris.

Start at her perineum and, with three fingers, move over her vagina. Your middle finger should move into her vagina slightly, while the other two move around the outside.

Rub around the clitoris gently, then imagine the clitoris is a compass and press on north, east, south, and west. Then press at northeast, northwest, southwest, and southeast.

Tease around the opening of her vagina then move one finger in and out very slowly.

Use your fingertips to massage the four internal vaginal walls. Alternate this with clitoral stimulation.

If she wants, bring her to climax in any way the two of you wish.

Finish by resting your hands on her vagina and heart as you did before.

Related Chapters:

- Touch

GETTING UNDRESSED

There are basically three ways to get naked: undress yourself, undress each other, or use a combination of the two. Whatever you choose, it's usually best to take your time.

Undressing each other can be as simple as taking turns removing items of clothing off each other, one item at a time. You could do this while dancing. Each time you expose a new piece of skin explore it with your hands, tongue, lips, etc. Brush erogenous zones if you're taking off pieces of clothing close to them.

Sample Routines for Undressing Your Lover

To undress her, come up from behind and kiss the back of her neck as you slide her dress off her shoulder. Unhook her bra by putting your thumb and forefingers on each side of the clasp and pushing into the center.

Cup her breasts and play with her nipples before sliding her bra down her shoulders.

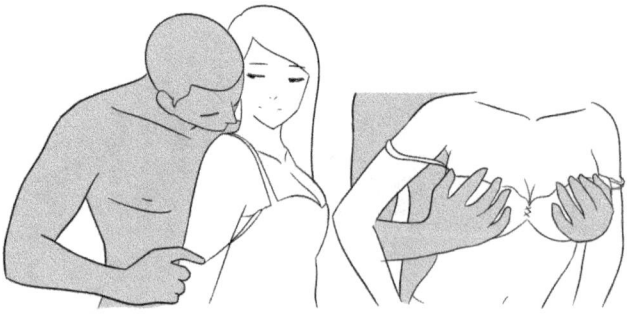

Kiss down her body until you are on your knees. Get in front of her and use your teeth to remove her panties.

To undress him, come in front of him and undo his shirt buttons from top to bottom, kissing his chest and/or stomach after each button is undone.

Do this until you are on your knees in front of him. Undo his fly and take his trousers off, following with your kisses. Slide your hands up his leg inside his underwear before pulling them down as well.

If you are the one being stripped, enjoy surrendering to your lover's control. Do not try to help. You can even dress up to be undressed—wear sexy underwear, leather, or a role-playing outfit, for example. You may find that you lover likes the outfit so much that you'll keep it on during sex.

Other Ideas for Undressing Each Other

- Just use your mouth.
- Only use your feet and toes.
- Make a game out of it, such as strip poker.
- Rip each other's clothes off.
- Undress while you are both blindfolded.

Stripping

To strip for your lover in a sexy way requires sensual movements while you slowly and seductively remove your clothes. Dim the lights and put on some music that you like to move to. It doesn't matter if you're not much of a dancer. Concentrate on the music and your lover's eyes, and just move. Dance around your lover emphasizing your assets, such as your chest, bum, or legs). Move close and put your leg up, rubbing your foot on your lover's crotch.

Start to remove your clothing, but don't just take things off. Take them off a little bit, then put them back on. Two steps forward, one step back. As each piece of clothing comes off, throw it in your lover's direction. Once you're down to your underwear, dance around without taking any more off for a little while. Come close to your lover, but don't let them touch you yet.

As your underwear comes off, brush it on your lover. You could tie their hands together, wrap it around their neck, brush it over their genitals, etc. Once you are completely naked, touch yourself provocatively while continuing to dance, ensuring your lover gets a good view. Do not let them touch until you are ready.

ORAL SEX

Oral sex can be enjoyed in all stages of sex. You can give your lover oral sex just for their pleasure (not to say you won't enjoy giving it), as foreplay, as a break from penetration during sex, or to bring your lover to orgasm if you climax first.

Whether giving or receiving, let your lover know that you are enjoying it. When giving, build anticipation. Undress your lover slowly, then kiss, lick, suck, nibble etc. anywhere on their body. Linger around the genitals before going in. You can even start while your lover is still asleep.

Different foods can be used to create a variety of sensations during oral sex. Filling your mouth with different things, such as mint, soda, jelly, marshmallows, or ice, will give your partner different sensations. Contrast—warm tea immediately followed by an ice cube, for example—feels great. Try covering your lover's genitalia with different foods for you to remove with your mouth.

Note: If you are going to be using a condom after wards, either wash first or only use water-based foods. No oil.

What you eat in everyday life will change the way you taste to your lover. Pepper and salt will make you bitter. Blander foods will give you a neutral taste, while sweet foods will make you sweet.

You can experiment using toys and/or masturbation techniques in conjunction with oral techniques.

Fellatio

Fellatio is when the man receives the oral sex. Since it can be done almost fully dressed, you can get away with it in a wider variety of places and times than you can with traditional intercourse. You can practice giving fellatio on a cucumber or similarly shaped object.

Find a comfortable position with your head between his thighs. There are many different variations. Either of you could be standing, lying on your back or front, sitting, kneeling, etc.

Caress his penis with your hands. Lick it occasionally in various ways. Use your whole tongue or just the tip on the entire length of his penis, treat it like a lollypop, flick your tongue on the head and perineum, circle the ridge with your tongue, etc.

Once he is very hard, either wet your lips and then extend your lips far beyond your teeth or wrap your lips over your teeth. Gently move your mouth up and down his penis, experimenting with different pressures, speeds etc. to discover what he enjoys the most. Allow saliva to flow freely. You can either keep your hands on his penis to help guide it where you want or just use your mouth.

As you continue to move your mouth up and down, there are many things you can do to further the stimulation. Mix it up so he doesn't know what is coming next.

- Lick his penis at the same time. You can rest the head of his penis on the roof of your mouth or in your cheek as you use your tongue. Use a pointed tongue to flick underneath the penis on his frenulum.
- When his penis is very wet try sliding it down your throat as far as you can (deep-throat). Your gag reflex may kick in. To prevent this, try to relax your throat and breathe through your nose. If you do gag, stop immediately; otherwise, you may vomit.
- Use different depths and/or rhythms
- Just suck on the head
- Suck on the way down, going down as far as you can.
- Hold the head of his penis in your mouth and circle your tongue around the head.
- Give him a hand job at the same time. Combine hand job

techniques with fellatio techniques, moving in the same way, in the opposite direction, or twisting.
- Join the tip of your finger with the tip of your thumb and place the ring it makes on the outside of your lips to give him a tighter fit.
- Fondle, lick, and/or suck his testicles. Don't suck the testicles too hard.
- Touch him everywhere.
- Cover the end of his penis, then press on the side of it with your lips and teeth.
- Put his penis in your mouth and clamp your lips together on it, then remove it from your mouth and do it again.
- Put half his penis into your mouth and actively suck and kiss it.

If he starts thrusting, it is a sign that he may be close to ejaculation and/or needs more stimulation. Increase speed and/or pressure and/or do the things he likes most. You can push down on his hips to control him. He may also try to guide your head. Let him know if it is too rough.

If you do not want him to ejaculate in your mouth you will have to finish him off with your hand. If he does ejaculate in your mouth, then you can either swallow it or discreetly spit it out.

Once he has climaxed, his penis may be very sensitive, so ease off. He may or may not want to kiss you afterward.

Cunnilingus

Cunnilingus is the act of giving the woman oral stimulation. If your tongue muscles tire easily, you can strengthen them by doing the following exercises daily in front of a mirror.

With a point in your tongue, move quickly from side to side in a steady rhythm. Next, do the same but move up and down instead of side to side. Finally, remove the point from your tongue and take long licks, focusing on the upward movement.Once your tongue is ready, it's time to do the real thing. Find a comfortable position so that your head is between her thighs. As with fellatio, there are many positions you can experiment with. Touch and kiss her all over her body, slowly moving to her groin.

When ready, use a wet finger to touch her labia, clitoris, and vagina. Kiss all around her groin, and finally, place your tongue on her vulva. Lick around the whole area. When ready, focus on her clitoris.

Use the following techniques at random. Pay attention to the techniques she likes the most. Every woman is different, so use her reactions (sounds, movement, etc.) as a guide.

Note: Do not touch or suck the clitoris too hard; otherwise, it will desensitize. Some women are very sensitive, and direct stimulation is too much. If this is the case, focus on the clitoral hood. If the clitoris "hides" under the clitoral hood, it is a good sign that you need to ease up on the pressure.

- With the tip of your tongue and using short strokes, repeatedly lick up the entrance of her vagina and over her clitoris.
- Lick only one side of the clitoral tip, then the other.
- Point your tongue and circle it around her clitoris.
- Use the tip of your tongue to repeatedly push on one side of the clitoral tip, then the other.
- Gently suck each of her labia, then her clitoris.
- Rapidly flicker the tip of your tongue all the way up her labia and over her clitoris.
- Point your tongue and use the tip to make circles on her clitoris. Keep a consistent rhythm.
- Lick up and down or back and forth on the clitoris.
- By putting your fingers in a scissor shape along her vulva, you can further expose her clitoris.

- Stroke her inner labia with your fingers as you lick her clitoris. Separate them with your fingers. Gently tug on them.
- Use your fingers or tongue to penetrate her vagina at the same time as you give her clitoral stimulation. Do it in rhythm.
- Use your hands to stimulate her whole body.
- Use the tip of your tongue to swirl and twirl around the top and sides of her clitoris.
- Swirl your tongue on her clitoris with your finger(s) in her vagina, rubbing or pressing on her G-spot.
- Give long licks with the flat of your tongue.
- Press on her perineum while stimulating her clitoris with your tongue.
- Suck her clitoris gently into your mouth. While maintaining the suction, push with your tongue.

Note: Never blow directly into the vagina.

To bring her to orgasm, use what she likes the most and keep a rhythm. Just like the penis, the clitoris may be very sensitive after orgasm, so ease off. After her climax, she may or may not want to cuddle, kiss, or move to other sexual acts.

Rimming

Rimming is oral sex for the anus. Ensure your partner's anus is clean and begin by circling your tongue around it, then lick up and down over it and flicker your tongue over the opening. Insert the tip of your tongue inside it a little to tease, and then continue on the outside and on the perineum. When ready, insert your tongue into the anus fully and move it around inside your lover. Humming will give your tongue a vibration.

Related Chapters:

- Touch
- Intercourse
- Masturbation

INTERCOURSE

Condoms and Lubricants

Using a condom is one of the easiest ways to protect against sexually transmitted diseases, and is also a very effective method of birth control. The use of condoms is highly recommended every time you have sex.

Some men feel that the use of condoms inhibits feeling. This can be a good thing if the man has a habit of climaxing too fast. If the case is the opposite, then special condoms (extra-thin ones, for example) can be used. There are also ribbed, flavored, fluorescent, and many other types.

Putting on a Condom

You can practice on a cucumber or similarly shaped object.

Extract the condom from its packet. Do not unroll it. Ensuring the condom is the right way around, unroll it down the erect penis using curved fingers. Squeeze the tip so it is air-free.

Using Your Mouth

Position the condom in your mouth so it is not visible. The opening should be facing your lover's penis in a way which it will enable you to unroll it the correct way. Place your mouth on his penis and move your mouth down his shaft, unrolling the condom as you go. Beware of your teeth.

Lubricants

Lubricants can be useful if the woman has problems with natural lubrication, if the man's penis is too big, during anal sex, or just for fun. You could cover yourselves in the lubricant and slide all over each other.

Like condoms, lubricants come in many types, some of which have special attributes. They may be tingling, warming, flavored, edible etc. If you are using lubricants during intercourse and are also using condoms, ensure the lubricants are water-based, so that they are compatible. Always use a natural substance which is made for the purpose. Baby oil, cooking oil, and many massage oils are not suitable as sexual lubricants.

Movement

There are many ways in which you can move other than the standard "in-out" thrusting. Try some of the following as well as experimenting with your own ideas and note what your lover responds to.

Note: Many of these suggestions come from the Kama Sutra and can be done by men or women.

- Vary the depth of penetration (deep, shallow, and midway).
- Vary the speed (faster or slower).
- Stop every now and again to kiss and caress your lover. This can also help for men who climax too quickly.
- Use different rhythms. If the standard rhythm is in-out-in-out, then try a short thrust in, short thrust out, deep thrust in, deep thrust out, then repeat. So the rhythm would be in-out-innn-ouut, in-out-innn-ouut. Experiment with different rhythms.
- Use body parts other than your hips to thrust. Arch your back, move your torso, etc.
- Take your penis in your hand and rub it against your lover's vagina. Rub along one side, on her clitoris, move it in circles inside her vagina, slap it against her vagina, press it against her vagina, etc.
- Enter her vagina from above.

- Thrust quickly and lightly.
- Go deep inside her vagina and move inside without withdrawing.
- Pushes while she withdraws, then withdraw while she pushes, and so on.
- Once you are inside her, both of you withdraw, keeping just the tip inside her, and then push together again.
- Thrust in sets. Do nine shallow thrusts, then eight shallow thrusts and one deep thrust, then seven shallow thrusts and two deep thrusts. Keep going in this manner until you reach nine deep thrusts.
- Stop completely for a full minute and become aware of thoughts and sensations.
- Have your lover mount you and move her internal muscles on your penis.
- Rub her clitoris while inside her.
- Enter her about an inch and just rest your penis there for a few minutes, feeling your energy. Use your penis to massage her clitoris and vaginal opening. After a few minutes, put your penis back inside her. Repeat this process several times. When you wish to climax, you can thrust slowly or continue to massage her clitoris.
- Have your lover lie on her back. Enter her, then moves up her body so the base of your penis rubs her clitoris. Go as high as you can without your penis slipping out. As she moves her pelvis down toward the bed, move yours toward the ceiling, and then come back together.

Sexy Getaway

Just being in an unfamiliar place can add a bit of spice to your sex life. You can rent a cottage in the woods, or go to a fancy hotel. Make a weekend (or week) out of it. Plan every moment with mutual consensus or just be spontaneous. Bring everything you will need for a weekend of sexual pleasure. While you're there, you can work on your tantra, or just make it a really dirty weekend, with no goal in mind but to have fun.

You don't have to go anywhere if you do not want to. You can have a sex holiday in the comfort of your own home, and for some, the hotel where you can pay by the hour triggers the sexual fiend inside them.

Where ever you decide to go, make sure it's conducive to you making a lot of noise.

Related Chapters:

- Massage

GETTING 'FREAKY'

Bondage

For some people it can be very stimulating to surrender to their lover. Bondage is a great way to do this. If you're new to bondage, then start slowly. Ask your lover to keep their hands over their head while you play just below the waistline. If/when your lover disobeys, use a soft material to bind their hands together. To progress further you can use blindfolds, restrain more body parts and perhaps move into S&M.

Note: Never leave your lover unattended while they are restrained.

Fantasies

It's normal and healthy to have sexual fantasies. You may feel that some are "bad." If some of your fantasies involve illegal activity, they are still OK; just don't act them out. You can talk about others with your lover, who may be more than happy to explore them with you, assuming they are the fantasies you want to live out.

Note: Never act out fantasies on an unwilling partner.

Many fantasies involve role-play (costumes often enhance the fantasy). Talk about what behaviors you are comfortable with during the role-play, then re-enact any fantasies your partner has. For example, they or you may wish to explore:

Service roles: Maid, waiter/waitress, slave, prostitute, butler, flight attendant, etc.

Power roles: Policeman and criminal, teacher and student, doctor and patient, model and photographer, etc.

Force fantasies: Aggressor and victim, domination, rape fantasies, etc.

Celebrity: Any celebrity or character you can think of.

Fetishes

A fetish is when someone gets sexually aroused by an otherwise non-sexual object or body part, such as certain clothes, feet, or leather. Fetishes are perfectly healthy to have, and are more common than most people think.

Exhibitionism

The thrill of possibly getting caught can be a big turn-on. Try the following places to have sex, and/or make up your own.

Note: Public sex is illegal in most places. Venture at your own risk.

- Outside (in the snow, in the pool, etc.).
- In the back of a taxi.
- At the drive-in.
- In the crowd at a rock concert.
- In the library.
- On swings at the playground.
- On a rollercoaster.
- At the beach.
- In the office.
- In a restaurant bathroom.
- On a plane.

Group Sex

Group sex is sexual interaction involving three or more people. Having more hands, mouths and sexual organs on and in your body can provide many different pleasurable experiences, not to mention the visual stimulation of watching others.

Swinging is when group sex is made into a sexual lifestyle rather than a one-off or occasional thing.

Group sex is not for everyone. There are physical and emotional aspects that require a certain sexual maturity. All participants should be 100% sure before trying it.

S&M

Sadomasochism is the act of exploring activities involving power or pain. One person is the dominant (the sadist), whilst the other is the submissive (masochist). It can be just during sex or in other areas of the relationship as well. It is a more hardcore version of role-playing and living out fantasy.

Note: If it is not consensual, it is abusive.

S&M practices can range from mild spanking to hardcore fisting and everything in between, including verbal humiliation, nipple clamps, piercing, hot wax, sensory deprivation, urination, and dog-leading. Whatever it is, never do anything without knowing how to do it safely, and be sure you talk about boundaries and behaviors before you begin.

Safe words can be used to help distinguish between pretend and real distress.

Outfits—rubber, PVC; glossy "server role" outfits such as maid and nurse uniforms, catsuits, bodysuits, outfits with holes cut in specific places, and many more—often play a big role in S&M.

Toys

There are many different sex toys that can be used either for masturbation or during sex with your lover(s). This chapter will give you a brief overview of what is available.

Vibrators

Vibrators come in many different shapes (tongues, penises etc.) and sizes (from very large to very discreet). Some are specifically designed for certain things, such as clitoral or simultaneous anal stimulation. They are usually battery-operated and many have different settings so you can choose the speed, rhythm, etc. of the vibration.

Dildos

Dildos are similar to vibrators, but are not powered. You can also get specifically designed dildos, including double-ended ones. Some come with a strap, so a woman can use them the way a man uses his penis.

Penis Sleeve

This is basically a fake vagina, mouth or anus. Add some lube.

Cock Rings

Specifically made for the man, these go over the penis. They may feel pleasing, as well as enabling the man to hold an erection for a longer time. These also come in vibrating versions.

Note: Cock rings are not a cure for erectile dysfunction, and should not be used as such. Do not use them if you are taking blood-thinning medication, if you suffer from nerve or vascular disease, or if you have diabetes.

Butt Plugs

These are specifically designed to give the anus a feeling of fullness. They are made from silicone or rubber, and are easy to clean. They come in a variety of shapes and sizes. The silicone versions are sensitive to vibration. Put a vibrator on the end to enhance the feeling.

Beads

There are a few different types of beads. Thai beads are small and are meant to be inserted into the anus. Most people get the enjoyment when they are pulled out. The speed at which they are pulled out gives various sensations. Jumbo beads are a larger version, and jelly beads are a spongy version.

Other Apparatus

There are many things that can be used in the name of kink: handcuffs, blindfolds, spanking paddles, collars and leads, nipple clamps, whips, sex swings, etc. Check out your local sex store or use an online catalog.

Anal Sex

Many people consider anal sex as taboo, which is often the appeal. It can also feel great. It usually offers a tighter fit for men, and many women orgasm from it. The male anus is also home to many pleasurable nerves.

Always wear a condom, use plenty of lubrication and take it very slowly.

Never swap from the anus back to the vagina without washing your penis and changing your condom.

To begin with, play gently with the outside of your lover's anus. Massage and press around the rim. Once the muscles relax, introduce very shallow penetration. Use the tip of your well-lubricated finger, for instance. When your lover is ready, begin to vary the depth and touch and gently work to widen the anus. The receiver must be relaxed. When you can fit at least two fingers in, you can slowly insert your very well-lubricated and erect penis. If it hurts, stop moving and just wait. It will take time for the anus to stretch to the point where penetration becomes painless and enjoyable.

There are many positions that are compatible with anal, but to begin with, the receiver may feel more comfortable and have more control by squatting over the penis. Anal penetration can also be introduced with sex toys such as butt plugs (ensure they have a flared base and are well lubricated) as well as during oral sex, when a finger or tongue can be inserted.

Whether using your finger, penis, tongue or a toy, don't forget about your lover's main sexual organ and other erogenous areas.

Related Chapters:

- Touch
- Oral Sex
- Masturbation

YOGA FOR BETTER SEX

INTRODUCTION

Yoga is amazing for sex, and is a low-impact way to maintain your body.

This routine in particular is specifically designed to:

- Increase sexual pleasure
- Alleviate sexual dysfunctions
- Intensify orgasms
- Increase sexual stamina

Even if you already have an exercise routine, you should add/include a yoga routine.

Some poses can be challenging. Adjust them to what you are capable of. Do your best and work your way up to them.

Never strain, and only remain in each position for as long as you want or as long as you feel comfortable.

CHAKRAS

Chakras are the energy centers in your body. Ideally, energy flows freely through them and in a balanced manner. When energy is not flowing freely, it leads to illness, emotional upset, etc.

The chakras are often referred to in yoga or tantric sex. From bottom to top, these are the names of the chakras and where they are located.

1st : Root/Base : Base of the spine.

2nd: Sacral : Lower abdomen.

3rd : Solar Plexus : Upper abdomen.

4th : Heart : Just above the heart.

5th : Throat : Throat

6th : Third Eye : Forehead between the eyes.

7th : Crown : Very top of the head.

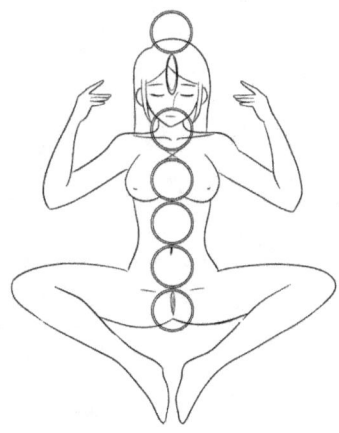

FULL-STOMACH BREATHING

Deep breathing is immensely beneficial in everyday life and an energy booster. It is also a key aspect of yoga, and is great during massage, foreplay, masturbation, and sex.

1. With your mouth closed, breathe in deeply through your nose. Count to four as you do so. Your ribs and stomach should expand as you fill up with air. As you inhale, imagine your body and chakras being filled with the clear, positive energies of love and happiness.
2. When you cannot breathe in any more, hold the breath for a count of two, then fully exhale to a count of four through your nose and/or mouth, pushing your stomach to your spine. Imagine all cloudy toxins, stress and negativity exiting your body.

Once in your pose (and while you adopt the pose), use full-stomach breathing and focus on the feelings in your chakras, especially the heart and base.

Related Chapters:

- Massage
- Chakras

SOLO YOGA ROUTINE

Mountain

Stand tall, with your feet shoulder-width apart. Spread your toes wide, straighten your legs, and draw your stomach in. Lift your chest, and roll your shoulders back keeping your head in line with your shoulders.

Standing Gentle Back Bend

Interlace your fingers and raise both arms over your head. Reach as high as you can. Look to your hands and bend back.

Side Bend

Drop one hand to your side and arc your other arm over your head, reaching to the side of the dropped hand. Repeat on your other side.

Bar-back

Keeping your legs, back and arms straight, place your hands on your thighs or knees. Roll your shoulders back and lift your head so you're looking straight ahead. Bend your knees if you need to.

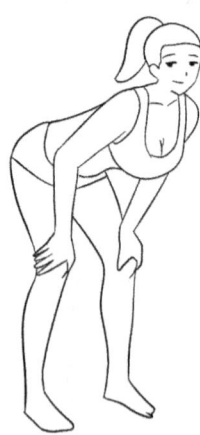

Spread-Leg Forward Bend

Stand with your feet facing forwards and approximately double shoulder-width apart. Keep your legs and back straight and bend forward at the hips. Aim to touch the floor with flat palms.

Ankle Grip

With your legs together, bend at the waist and grab the back of your calves or ankles. Keep your legs straight and pull your chest towards your knees.

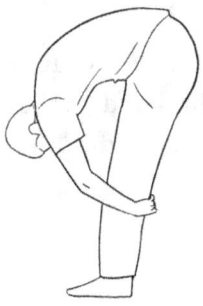

Eagle

Cross your right elbow over your left elbow and bring your left fingertips toward the base of your right palm. Bring your right leg over your left and tuck your right foot behind your left ankle. Fix your gaze to help with balance, and lift your elbows straight up toward the sky. Swap sides.

Prayer Twist

Stand with your feet together. Put your palms together as if praying. Keeping your back straight, bend at the knees and bring your left elbow to the outside of your right knee. Look up over your right shoulder. Swap sides.

Downward Facing Dog

Get on your hands and knees, with your hands shoulder-width apart and fingers facing forwards. Keeping your arms straight, come up onto your feet. Keep your feet facing forward and shoulder-width apart. Relax your neck, straighten your legs, and press your heels down. Your final position should be an inverted V.

*** From Three-Legged Dog to Opener is a set which is repeated on the other side ***

Three-Legged Dog

From Downward-Facing Dog, raise your right leg as high up as you can while keeping it straight.

Forward Lunge

Bring your raised right leg down with your foot flat next to your right hand. Your left leg should stay straight.

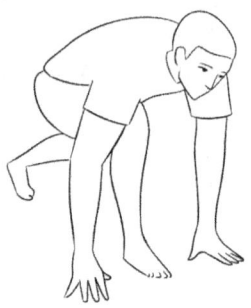

Ankle Wraps

Bring your right hand in front of your right ankle, then wrap around it counterclockwise. Your left hand should down so that you are grabbing your ankle with both hands.

When you're ready, keep your left hand wrapped around your ankle and raise your right arm to the sky. From here, drop your right hand behind your back, and clasp your hands together. Lean your head back.

Warrior

Go back into the Forward Lunge, then straighten your back vertically and raise your hands to the sky. Look to your hands.

Back Lunge

Keep your right hand up and then slide your left hand down your left thigh. Your left leg should stay straight and your right leg should stay bent.

Side Twist

Go back into Warrior, then drop your right hand to the floor next to your right foot on the outside. Your left hand should go high into the air. Look up at your left hand.

Reverse Side Twist

Go back into Warrior. Drop your left hand to the floor next on the inside of your right foot. Your right hand should go high in the air. Look to your right hand.

Triangle

Go back into Warrior, then straighten your right leg. Keep your left arm up and place your right hand onto your right shin. Keep your head aligned with your right foot. Look to your left hand.

Reverse Triangle

Go back into Warrior. Keep your right hand up and reach your left arm forward to place it on your right shin. Press down on your left hand while looking up to your right hand.

Opener

Place your hands back on the floor directly underneath your shoulders. Put your right foot close to your left hand. Lower your left knee to the floor, allowing your right knee to drop to the floor behind your right hand, so that you are on your right glute. Lift your chest, roll your shoulders back, and look up as you press your palms into the ground.

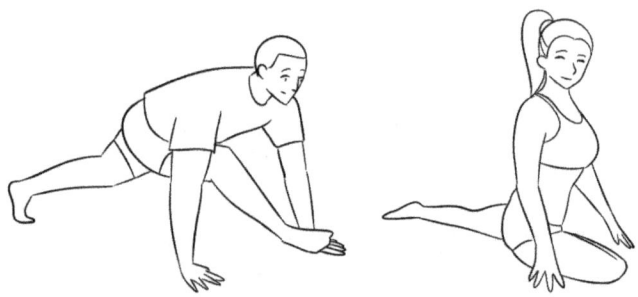

When you're ready, reach your arms forward, aiming to put your chest on the floor. Press your left hip forward and your right hip down and back.

*** **Repeat from Downward-Facing Dog on your left side** ***

Crane

Squat down, with your feet a few inches apart. Place your hands on the floor in front of you, shoulder-width apart. Your elbows should be on the insides of your knees. Lean forward and bring your feet off the floor. Your knees should balance on your elbows. Keep the soles of your feet together.

Reverse Crane

Stand straight and cross your feet. Squat down to create a gap between your knees. Place your hands on the floor, so that your elbows are on the insides of your knees with your hands on the outside of your ankles. Do not lock your elbows. Balance on your hands.

Cobra

Lie flat on your stomach, with your legs straight back and the tops of your feet on the floor. Press your palms into the floor to lift your chest. Roll your shoulders back and look up.

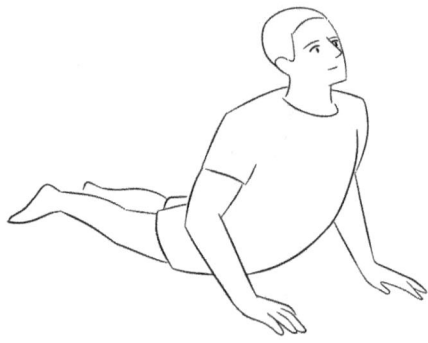

Cat Lift

Get on your hands and knees. Your hands should be directly beneath your shoulders. Look up and arch your back, pressing your stomach towards the floor.

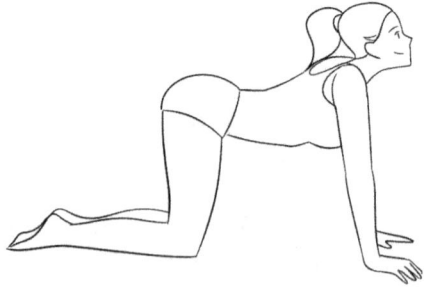

Cat Arch

Drop your head and arch your back, raising it to the sky. Suck your stomach to your spine.

*** From Two-Legged Table to Outstretched Table is a set which is repeated on both sides ***

Two-Legged Table

Make your back level. Extend your left foot straight back and your right arm straight forward. Engage your leg and arm muscles.

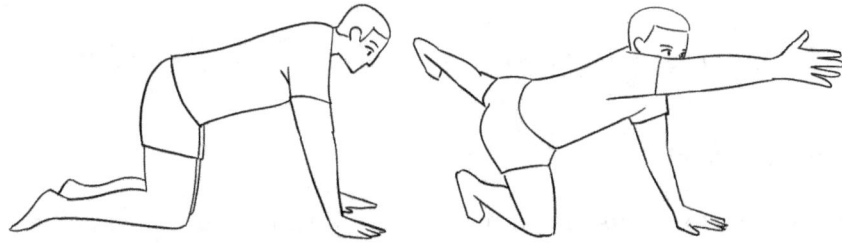

Twisted Table

Bend your left knee and grab your left ankle with your right hand.

Outstretched Table

Straighten your left leg and hold it out to the left while holding your right arm straight out to your right.

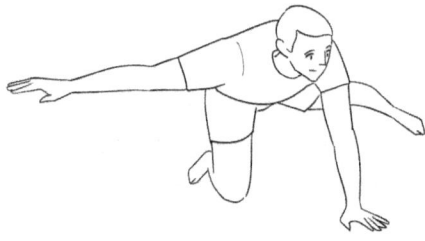

*** Repeat from Two-Legged Table on your other side ***

Forward Plank

Place your forearms flat on the floor, with your palms open and flat on the floor as well. You should be on your toes. Tighten your abdomen, back, buttocks, and legs.

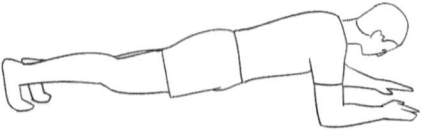

Side Planks

Lie on your side, propped up on your forearm, so that your head, torso, and feet are aligned. Your supporting elbow should be under your shoulder and in line with your hips, knees and feet.

Push up on your supporting elbow to lift your hips off the floor. Raise your arm towards the sky and look at your hand. Keep your rib cage lifted and your shoulder down.

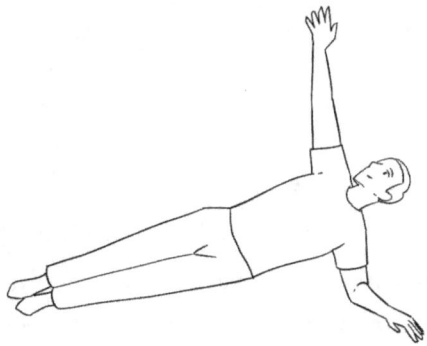

Next, support yourself on your hand instead of your forearm. Finally, raise your top leg to the sky.

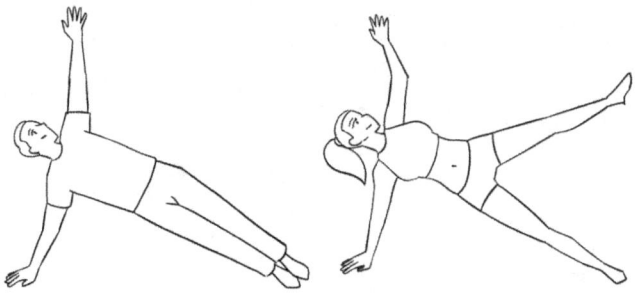

Repeat on your other side.

Frog

Lie flat on your belly. Bend your knees outwards on the floor. Prop your upper body up with your forearms. Your hands should be in a prayer position. The insides of your feet and knees should press on the floor. Bring your hips as close to the floor as possible.

Camel

Kneel on the floor with your knees shoulder-width apart. Arch backward and grab your heels with your hands. Look behind you.

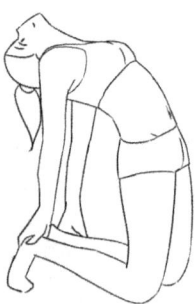

Forward Hero

Straighten your back and sit so your bum is on the floor, on the inside of your heels. Raise your arms straight above your head. Exhale and lean forward so your hands touch the floor, keeping your bum on the floor as well.

Fish

Lie on your back and put your hands under your bum. Press your forearms and elbows on the floor, lifting your upper torso and head off the floor. Rest the top of your head on the floor, but don't let it bear weight. You can also raise your feet off the floor. Keep your legs straight.

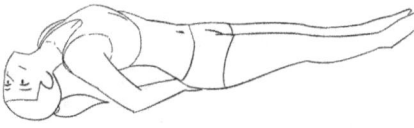

Lying-Down Leg Raises

Lie on your back and raise your leg, while keeping your other leg on the floor. With both hands, grab your leg as close to your ankle as you can and pull it towards your shoulder. Keep your legs as straight as you can. Repeat on the other side.

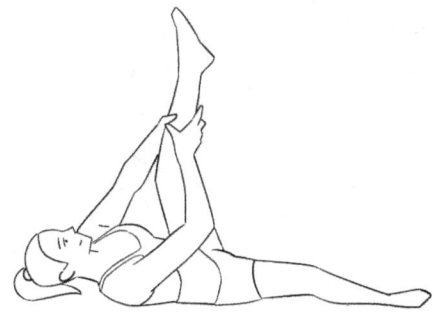

Shoulder Stand

Lie on your back, with your legs together. Keep your legs straight and roll back onto your shoulders. Use your hands on your back for support. Extend your legs and feet to the sky. Only your head, shoulders, upper arms, and elbows should touch the floor.

Plow

Keeping your legs straight, extend them behind your head, trying to touch your toes on the floor behind you. Lower your arms to the floor, parallel to your torso. Keep your neck off the floor by keeping your chin away from your chest.

Sleeping Angel

With your feet in the air and your legs straight, spread your legs and grab your big toes. Keep your neck off the floor.

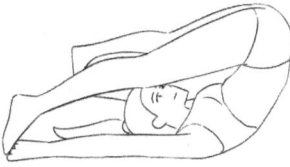

Dead Bug

Lie flat on your back and bring your knees up so the soles of your feet face the sky. With your elbows on the inside of your knees, grab the outside of each foot. Pull your knees toward the floor.

Lying Twist

Extend your arms to your sides and let your knees drop to the right while you look over your left shoulder. Cross your right ankle over your left knee and use it to press your left knee towards the floor.

Knee Pull

With your right ankle still crossed over your left knee, grab your left knee and pull it to your chest. Relax your neck and shoulders and let your tailbone sink to the floor.

*** Repeat Lying Twist and Knee Pull on your other side ***

Bridges

If you are on hard ground, use something to provide padding for your head, such as a folded towel.

Lie on your back, with your arms parallel to your body. Bend your knees so your feet are flat on the floor. Keeping your head, neck, arms and shoulders on the floor, push with your legs and arch your back to lift your stomach to the sky.

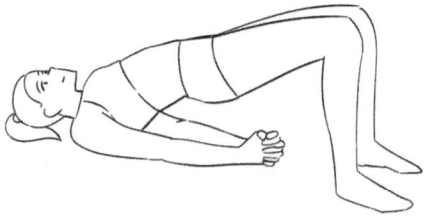

Next, place your hands flat on either side of your head. Place your feet on the ground and use them to push yourself into an arched back position, rolling on your head. Attempt to touch your nose to the floor.

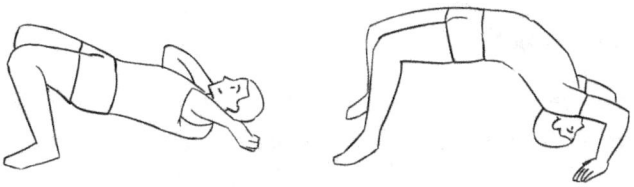

Finally, push up on your hands to raise your head off the floor.

Forward Fold

Sit on the floor with your back straight and your legs straight out in front of you. Your feet should be together, with your toes pointing to the sky. Reach for your toes and pull your chest to your knees.

Seated Open Angel

Spread your legs as far as you can. Grab your big toes with the first two fingers of each hand. Keep your back straight and press your hips forward.

Seated Angel

Sit back up and bring the soles of your feet together. Interlock your fingers around your two big toes. Bring your feet as close to your body as possible. Keep your back straight and relax your knees toward the floor.

Supine Angel

Lie on your back while keeping the soles of your feet together. Rest your hands on your lower abdomen.

Corpse Pose

Straighten your legs, pin your shoulders to the floor, and let your hands fall by your sides, palms facing up. Concentrate on deep stomach breathing or do any other meditation you like.

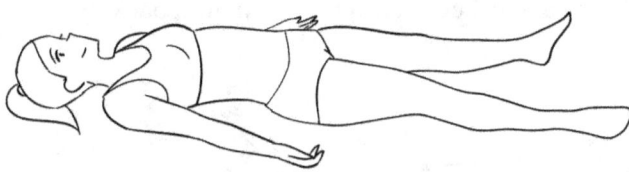

Related Chapters:

- Breathing

PARTNERED YOGA ROUTINE

Any method of exercising together helps to create a deeper connection. This is especially true with partnered yoga, where you will often breathe in sync and feel/concentrate on each other's energy.

If you are feeling a bit friskier, you can do the poses naked and see how far you can get before losing control. After all, many of them are taken straight from the Kama Sutra.

The poses are presented in a particular order which you can follow, but feel free to do what you wish.

Note: Many of these descriptions refer back to poses from the Solo Yoga Routine chapter.

Driving the Peg Home

Stand facing each other, bodies touching. Grab each other around the waist and use each other as support. Both arch back.

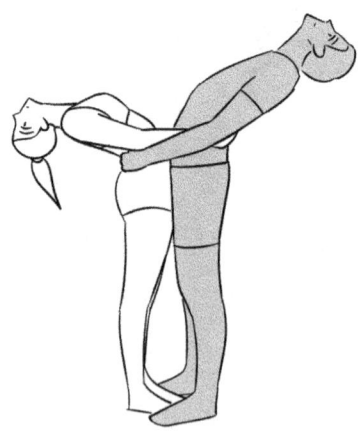

Lovers Pelvis Press

Stand facing each other, feet shoulder-width apart and about a foot away from each other. Both arch back with your hands high in the air, pressing your groins together for support.

Dangling Lovers

Stand facing each other, hands together. Step apart while letting your upper torsos dangle to the floor. Keep your legs straight, with your hands meeting in the center between you.

Squat-to-Stand Support

Squat down while facing each other. Hold each other's wrists and keep your backs straight. Support each other as you stand up together.

Seated Open Angels

You are both in a modified Seated Open Angel. Get close enough so your feet are touching and grab each other's wrists. Lean back to help stretch your partner stretch forward, then vice versa.

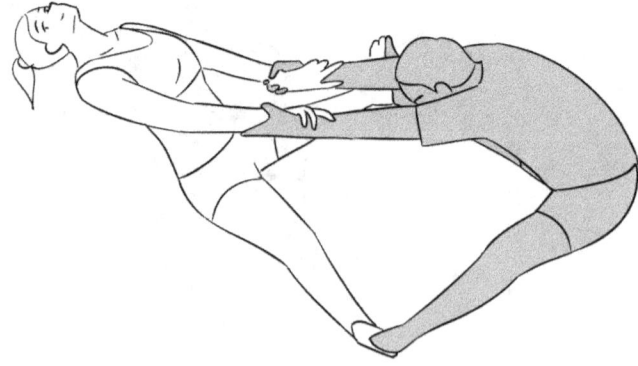

Raised Seated Open Angels

Sit as if in Seated Open Angels, but with your legs not stretched out as far. Hold hands on the outside of your legs and bring your legs up.

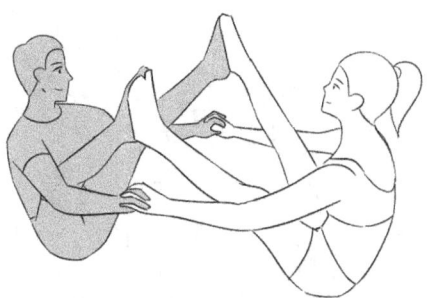

Cobras

Lie flat on your stomachs with your heads touching. With your hands under your shoulders, push your bodies up, arching your backs and looking to the sky.

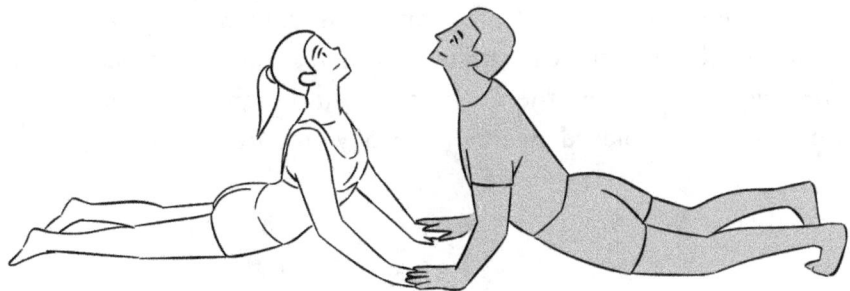

Kama's Wheel

Sit in Seated Angel. Your partner should sit in front of you, also in Seated Angel, and up against your groin. Wrap your arms around your partner and hold their ankles while they hold your feet.

White Tiger Tao

Your partner adopts Frog. Come from behind, with your legs in Frog on top of them. Your legs should alternate, and your groin should press against your partner. Support your weight on your hands, which should be placed on either side of your partner's hips.

Congress of the Cow

Your partner is on their hands and knees. Their knees are shoulder-width apart under her hips, and her hands are directly underneath her shoulders. Her arms are straight. She arches her back, pushing her stomach out whilst looking up to the sky. Get behind her on your knees and press your groin against hers. Place your knees between her legs. Go into an improvised Camel, using her feet as support.

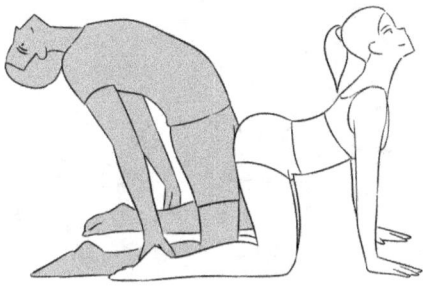

Lovers Embrace

Your partner adopts the Forward Hero. Kneel close behind her, one knee on either side of her body. Leans over her, pressing his body against hers. Positions can be swapped.

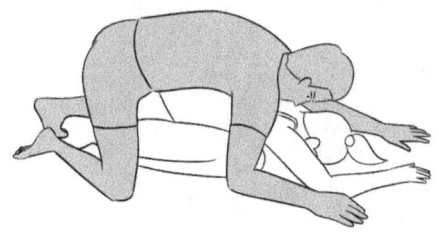

Mill Vanes

Your partner lies in Supine Angel. You adopt a modified Frog on top of them. You are facing away from her, with your legs on either side of her body. You use your hands for support, and rest your groin against theirs. Their hands rest on your bum.

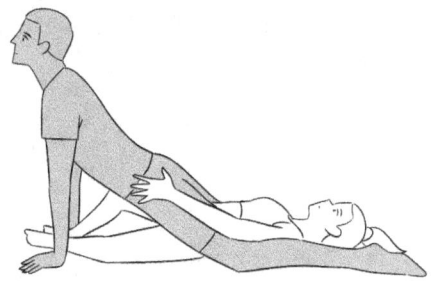

Amazon

You lie on your back and bring your knees to your chest. Your partner faces you, and you hold hands. Their feet are on either side of your hips and your legs are on either side of their torso. They squat down, bringing their groin to yours.

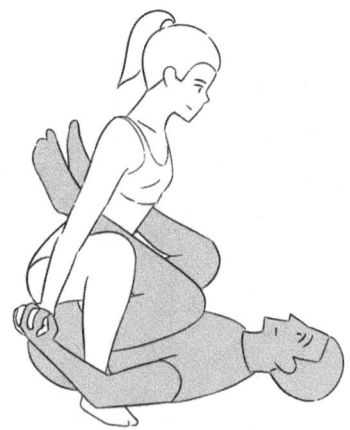

Ascending

You adopt Fish. Your partner places their knees on either side of you, so that their groin is on yours. Their hands rest on their calves, and their head on your chest.

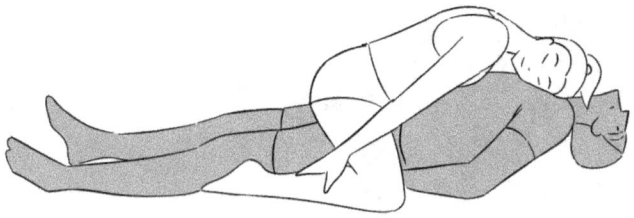

Arc

Your partner goes into the Bridge. You kneel between their legs, pressing your groin against theirs. You support them at the small of their back while they come up on the top of their shoulders. Their hands rest on your calves.

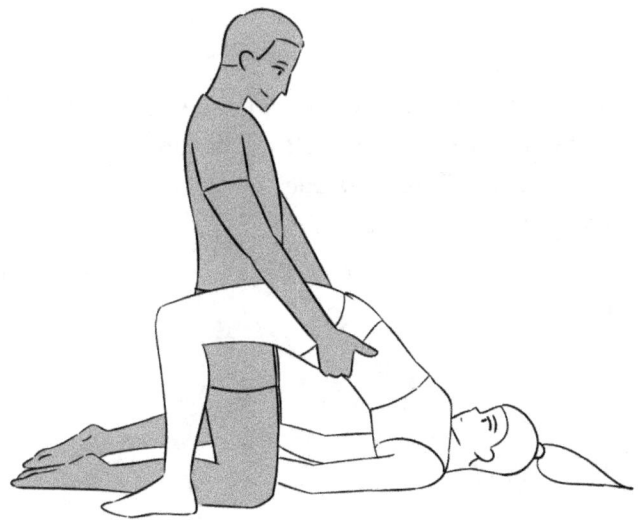

Anango-Rango

You squat with your feet double shoulder-width apart. Your partner does a back bend in such a way that their legs are on either side of your waist. Their hands are on the floor in front of you, fingers facing back towards you and eyes forward, away from you. Their legs dangle over your thighs.

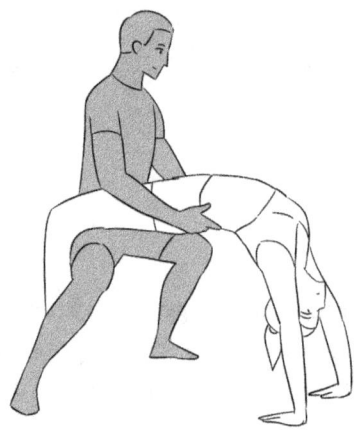

Twining

You partner performs a lying down leg raise with their left leg in the air. You face her and brings your left leg beyond their head on their right side. Your right leg stretches back on the inside of their right leg. Your groins are pressed together.

Wife of Indra

Your partner adopts Plow while you take up Camel. You touch at your groins. Your partner holds you by the back of your thighs.

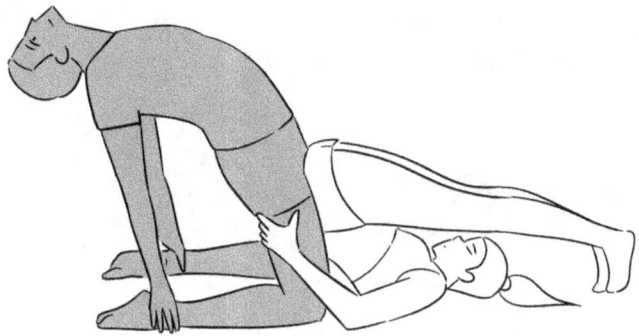

Clasping

Your partner lies on their back with their legs spread. You put your groin to theirs, keeping your body straight and supporting your weight on your toes and hands. You partner crosses their ankles around your waist. You press your hips down, pushing your upper body up off the floor at the same time.

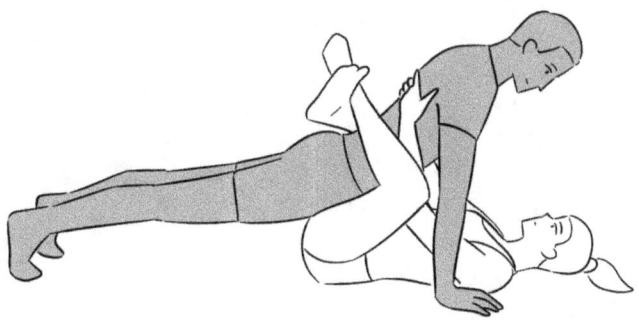

Face to Face

Your partner lies flat on their back, legs spread. You lie on top of them. Your groin rests on theirs. Your legs are straight and your feet are together. You support your weight on your toes. You and your partner grab each other's hands. You push down with your hips while lifting your upper body.

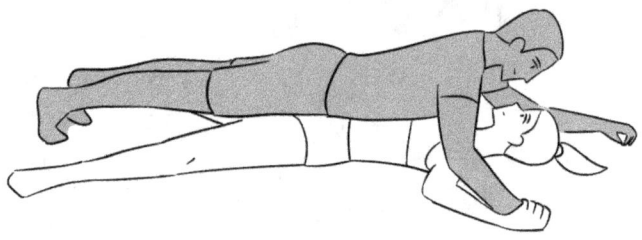

Related Chapters:

- Solo Yoga Routine

SOLO YOGA ROUTINE QUICK LIST

- Mountain
- Standing Gentle Back Bend
- Side Bend
- Bar-back
- Spread Leg Forward Bend
- Ankle Grip
- Eagle
- Prayer Twist
- Downward Facing Dog
- Three Legged Dog
- Forward Lunge
- Ankle Wraps
- Warrior
- Back Lunge
- Side Twist
- Reverse Side Twist
- Triangle
- Reverse Triangle
- Opener
- Crane
- Reverse Crane
- Cobra
- Cat Lift
- Cat Arch
- Two Legged Table
- Twisted Table
- Outstretched Table
- Forward Plank
- Side Planks
- Frog
- Camel
- Forward Hero
- Fish
- Lying Down Leg Raises
- Shoulder Stand
- Plow
- Sleeping Angel
- Dead Bug
- Lying Twist
- Knee Pull
- Bridges
- Sitting Stretch
- Seated Open Angel
- Seated Angel
- Supine Angel
- Dead Man

PARTNERED YOGA ROUTINE QUICK LIST

Driving the Peg Home

Lovers Pelvis Press

Dangling Lovers

Squat to Stand Support

Seated Open Angels

Raised Seated Open Angels

Cobras

Kama's Wheel

White Tiger Tao

Congress of the Cow

Lovers Embrace

Mill Vanes

Amazon

Ascending

Arc

Anango-Rango

Twining

Wife of Indra

Clasping

Face to Face

126 SEX POSITIONS GUARANTEED TO SPICE UP YOUR BEDROOM

INTRODUCTION

What follows are descriptions of many different positions for you to experiment with. They are grouped into similar positions: from behind, man on top, woman on top, etc. Many can be adapted to masturbation, toy play, and anal sex.

While experimenting, consider the following:

- Where the woman's vagina is too big for the man's penis, use positions where she can grip his penis, or where her legs are drawn to her chest to allow for deeper penetration. Positions where her feet are crossed will make her vagina tighter on his penis.
- If the man is too big for the woman, use positions that do not allow him to penetrate too deeply.

MAN ON TOP

Man-on-top positions allow for face-to-face contact, which is highly intimate. They also give the highest percentage of women orgasms, and are the best for inducing pregnancy.

Some of these positions may be uncomfortable for women who are already pregnant, or when men are too heavy for women.

POSITION 1. 1ST POSTURE

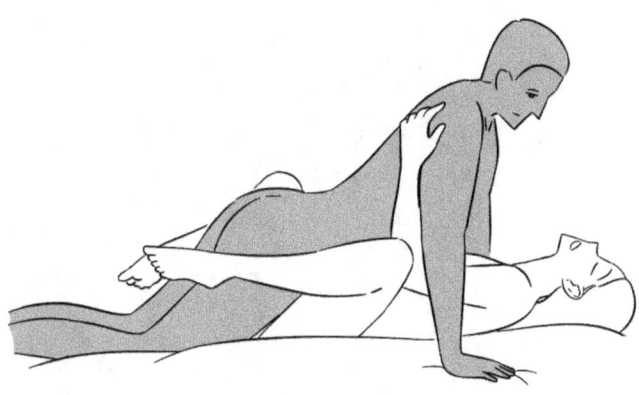

She lies on her back, with her knees pulled back and her legs spread. He lies in between her legs and supports himself on his arms. She can wrap her feet around his thighs. He can enter her at a high angle for clitoral stimulation.

POSITION 2. 2ND POSTURE

She lies on her back and puts her legs in the air. She grabs her ankles, which opens her up. He rests his weight on his hands, which are placed on either side of her head.

POSITION 3. 3RD POSTURE

He kneels in between her legs. One of her legs goes over his shoulder on the same side (e.g., her right leg on his left shoulder). Her other leg is relaxed near his waist and under his arm.

POSITION 4. 4TH POSTURE

He kneels. She lies on her back and puts her legs on either side of his head. She rests the undersides of her knees on his shoulders.

POSITION 5. BRIDAL BRIDGE

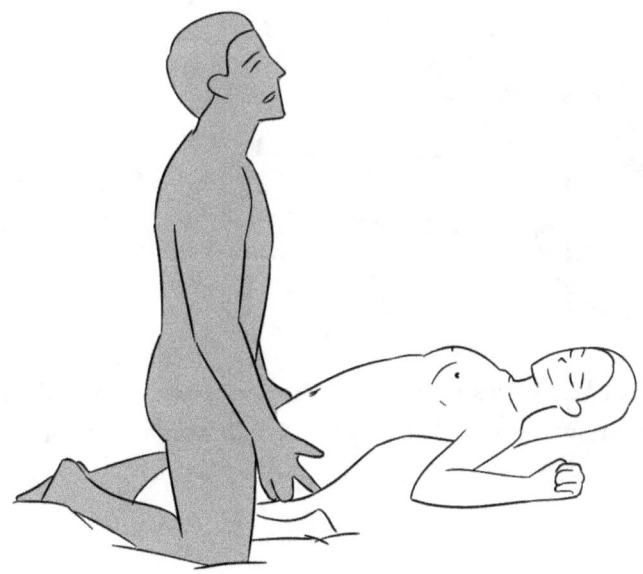

She gets on her knees and lies back onto some pillows. He kneels in front of her, his knees on the outside of hers.

POSITION 6. BACKWARD BENDING FLOWER

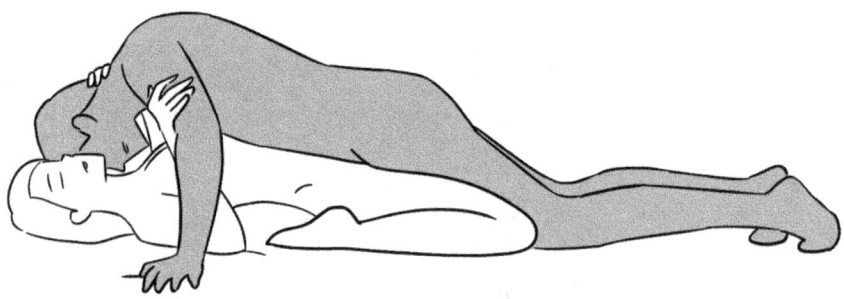

She gets on her knees and lies all the way back. A pillow under her lower back may increase her comfort. He lies on top of her.

POSITION 7. 7TH POSTURE

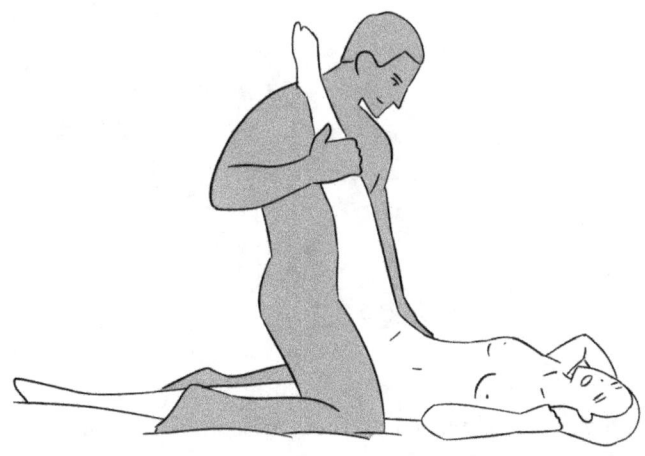

She lies on her back, slightly to one side. He is kneeling. One of her legs is on his shoulder, while the other is straightened underneath him. His knees rest on either side of her grounded leg.

POSITION 8. 8TH POSTURE

She lies on her back with her feet crossed. He is on top, with his knees on either side of her. He supports his weight on his hands and knees.

POSITION 9. APE

He kneels. She lies on her back and rests her calves on his shoulders. He lifts her by the hips onto his penis.

POSITION 10. 10TH POSTURE

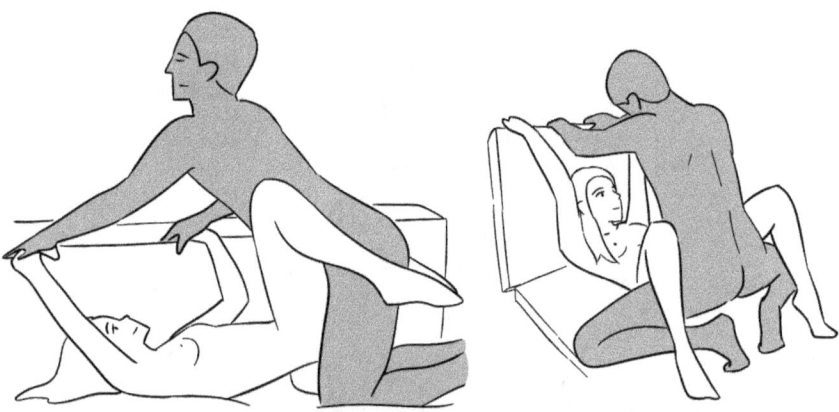

She lies on her back and raises her arms to grab something behind her head, such as the headboard. He is on his knees in between her legs, and he also grabs the headboard. She can raise her hips to meet him or plant her feet on the floor. They can push and pull against whatever they are holding onto.

POSITION 11. 11TH POSTURE

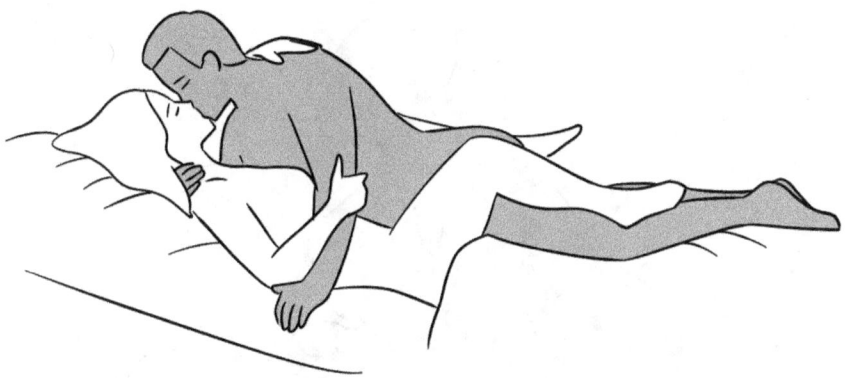

She lies on her back with her legs apart and he lies on top of her, in between her legs. Her feet are on the backs of his calves, and her legs are relaxed. She can press her feet together for a tighter fit.

POSITION 12. LEVEL-FEET

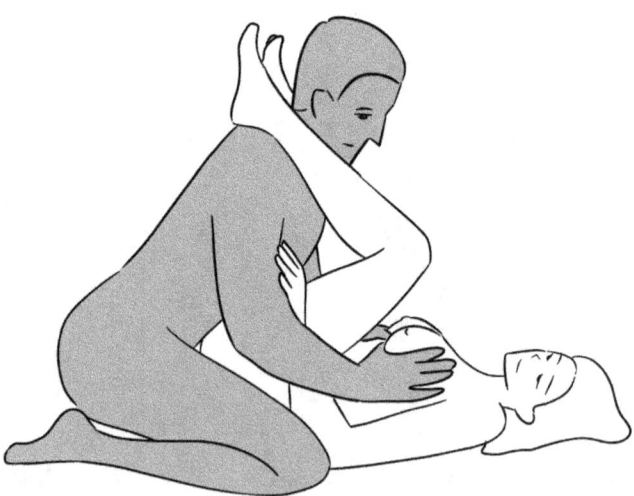

She lies on her back and places her legs on his shoulders, one on either side of his head. He kneels with his legs on either side of her, sitting on his calves.

POSITION 13. PINE TREE

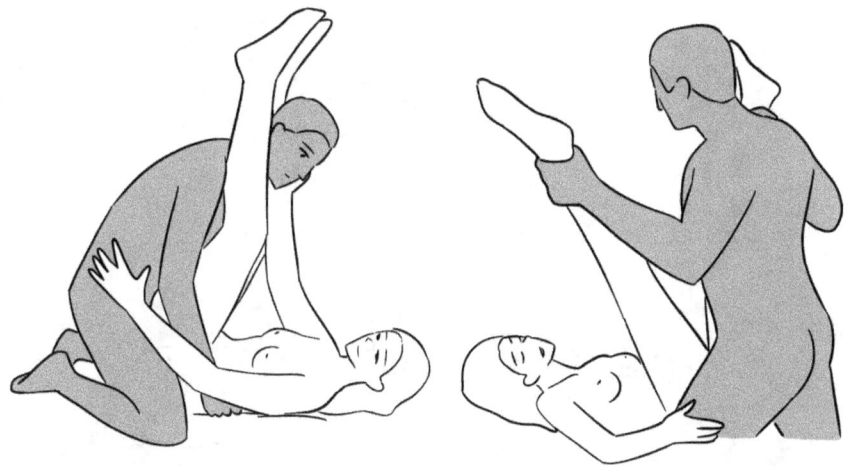

She raises her legs high in the air, one on either side of his head. He kneels up against her. He needs to be careful not to push her legs too far forward. From here, she can spread her legs as he grabs her ankles.

POSITION 14. RISING STAR

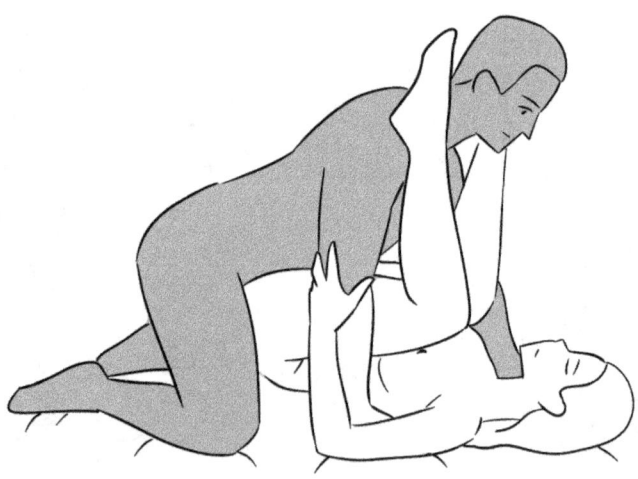

She lies on her back, with a pillow under the small of it. She brings her knees to her chest. He kneels in front of her with his knees on either side of her. He leans forward on her, resting his weight on his hands.

POSITION 15. SPLITTING

She lies on her back, with her legs together and in the air. He kneels in front of her, one knee on either side of her. She rests both her legs on one of his shoulders. pressing her knees and thighs together. He can hold her around the knees or come up higher and grab around her calves. She can cross her legs for a tighter fit and he can lean in for deeper penetration.

POSITION 16. TAIL OF THE OSTRICH

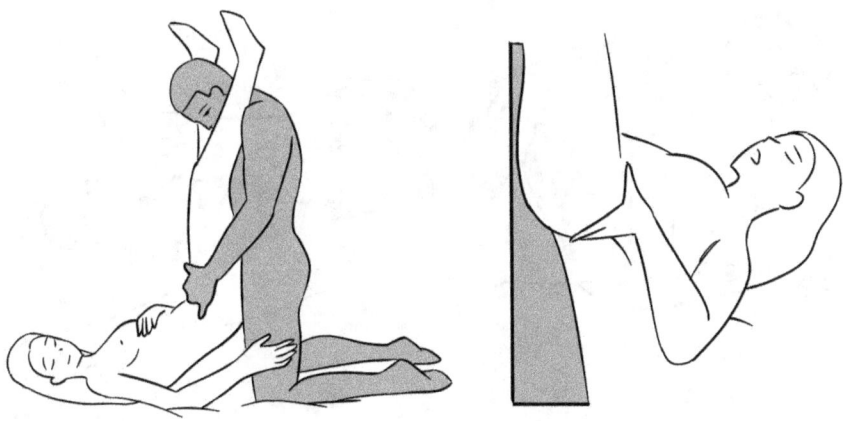

She lies on her back with her legs straight in the air and resting on his shoulders, one on either side of his head. He is on his knees in front of her, in a tall posture. She raises her hips, using her hands if needed.

POSITION 17. SWALLOWS IN LOVE

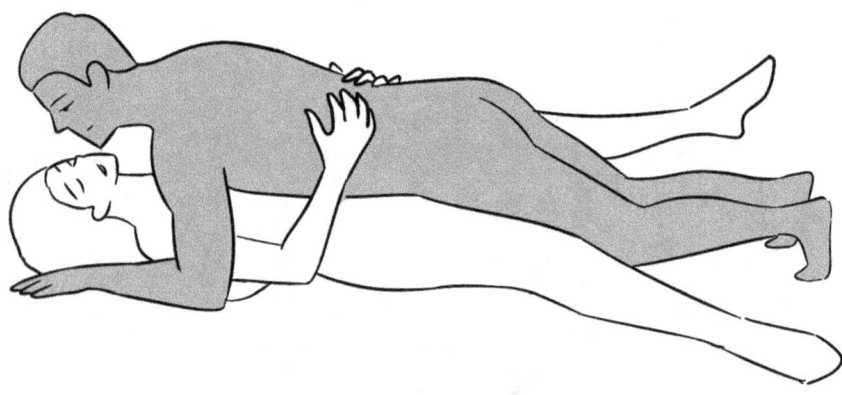

She lies on her back completely flat and relaxed, with her legs slightly apart and fairly straight. He is on top, with his legs in between hers. He rests on his elbows.

POSITION 18. YAWNING

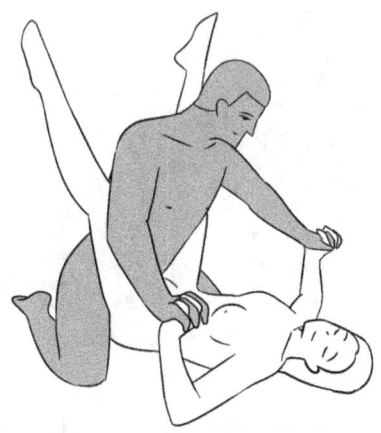

She lies on her back, with her feet high in the air and her legs open. He kneels in between her legs and they join hands. Her legs are at his waist level. He must be careful not to thrust too hard. She can invite deeper penetration by bringing her knees to her chest.

As a variation, she rests her legs on his shoulders and they place their hands on the floor on either side of her head.

He can also lean in closer and she can hold his waist.

POSITION 19. DRAGON TURNS AWAY

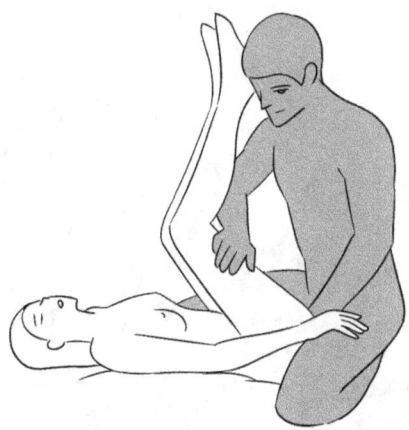

She lies on her back with her legs in the air. He moves them to one side and kneels, with one knee on either side of her.

POSITION 20. G-SPOT STIMULATOR

She lies on her back and places her legs on his shoulders, one on either side of his head. He is on his knees up against her. She raises her buttocks so he can enter her.

POSITION 21. CRAB

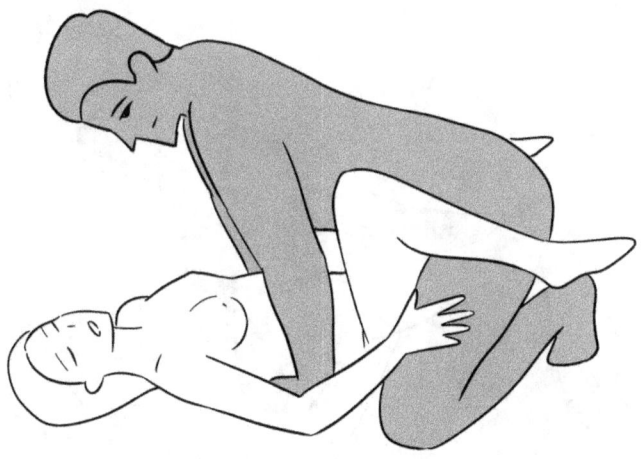

She lies on her back and bends her knees so her feet are off the floor. He kneels, with his knees on either side of her body, and supports his weight on his hands.

POSITION 22. DRAGON TURN

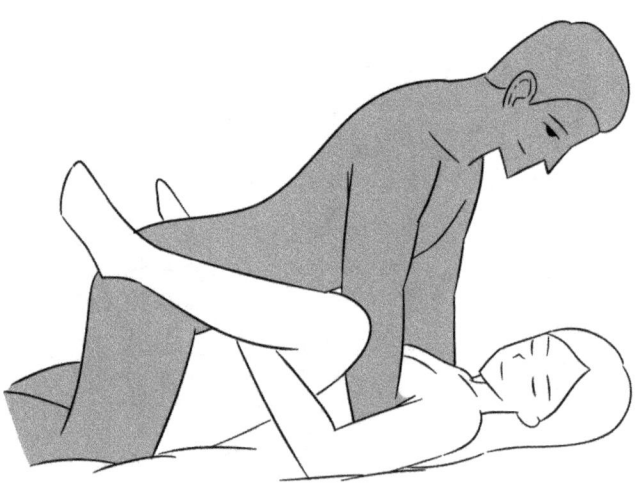

She lies on her back, draws her knees towards her chest, and uses her hands to pull them apart. He is on his knees, with his body in between her legs, and places his knees on either side of her buttocks. He rests his weight on his hands and knees.

POSITION 23. GALLOPING HORSE

She lies on her back with her feet planted on the floor. He kneels in between her legs. She raises her hips onto him. He holds her by the ankle and the neck.

POSITION 24. GAPING

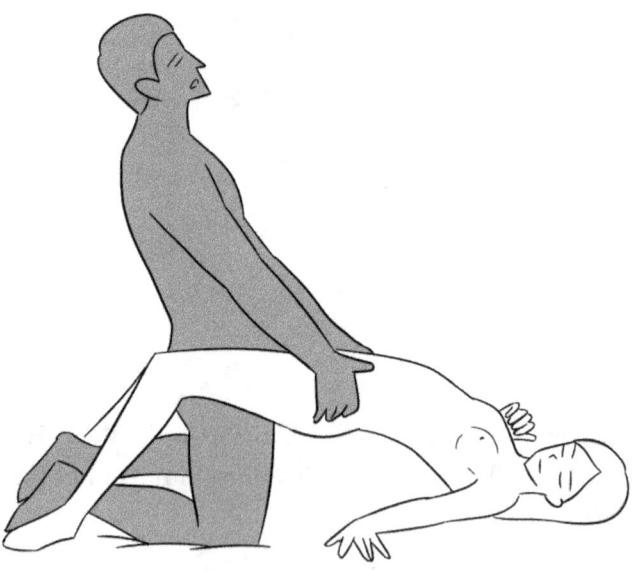

She is on her back. He kneels between her legs. She arches her back to meet his groin and can continue to move her hips up to meet his thrusts. Only her head, arms, the tops of her shoulders, and her feet touch the floor.

POSITION 25. GRIPPING WITH TOES

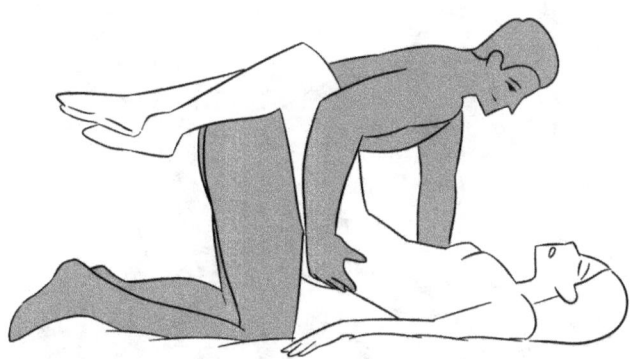

She lies on her back. He kneels in between her legs and uses his arms to help support his weight. She raises her hips to meet his groin and crosses her ankles around his waist, so she can use her legs to raise and lower herself on his penis.

POSITION 26. HUGE BIRD ABOVE A RED SEA

She lies on her back and draws her knees towards her chest. He kneels in between her legs. Her legs go over his arms. He leans forward and raises her buttocks to his groin.

POSITION 27. ONE WHO STOPS AT HOME

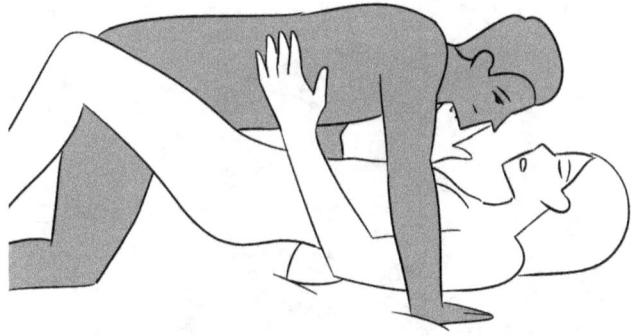

She lies on her back, with him on his knees between her legs. He helps support his weight on his hands. She lifts her pelvis up and down on his penis.

POSITION 28. PLACID EMBRACE

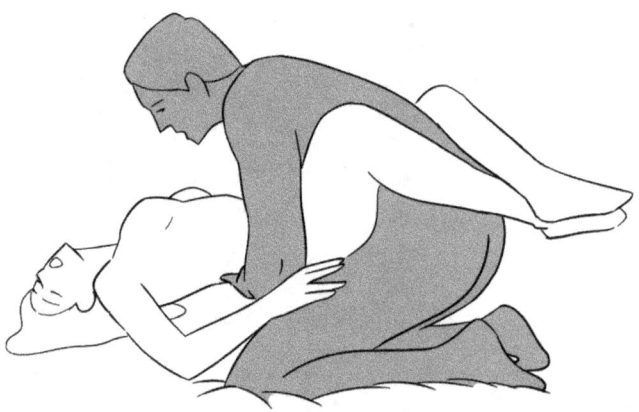

She lies on her back and he kneels in between her legs. He pulls her up onto his groin and she crosses her legs around his back. She pulls him in with her legs and he helps to support her weight with his arms.

POSITION 29. PRESSING

She is on her back and he lies in between her legs, using his arms to support himself. She grips him with her thighs, tightening her vaginal muscles on his penis.

POSITION 30. RAISED FEET

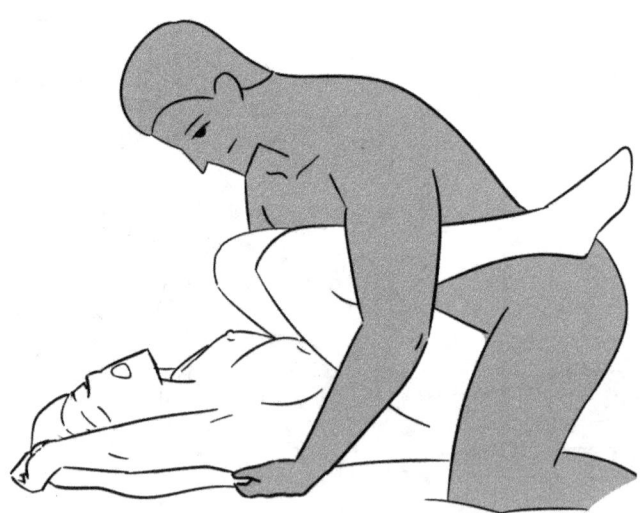

Lying on her back, she bends her legs at the knees and draws them back. He enters her from a kneeling position. They can enhance this position by placing some cushions under her bum. She can pull him closer with her legs.

POSITION 31. REFINED POSITION

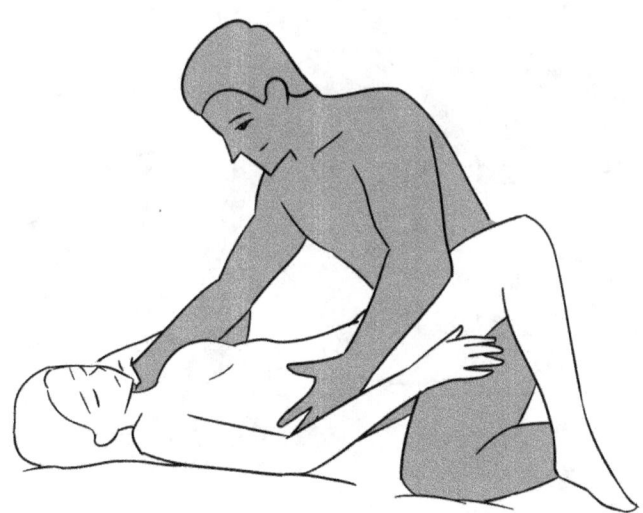

She lies on her back and he kneels in between her legs. Her feet are planted on the floor. She raises her hips to meet his groin.

POSITION 32. SILKWORM SPINNING A COCOON

She is flat on her back and he lies in between her legs, supporting his weight on his hands. She wraps her legs tightly around his torso, then raises and lowers her hips in time with his thrusts.

POSITION 33. STOPPERAGE

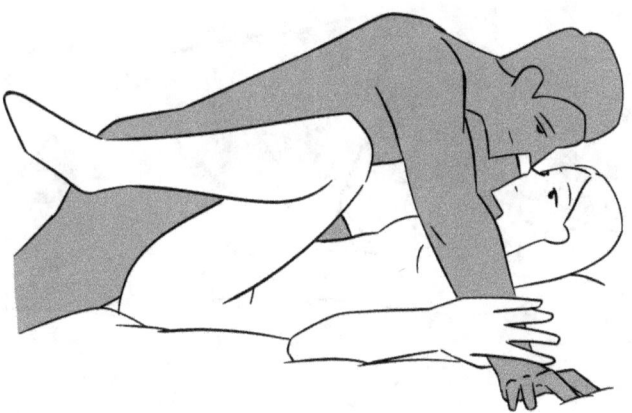

She lies on her back and brings her knees towards her chest. He kneels between her legs, bringing his face close to hers while supporting his weight on his hands. She can draw him in by pressing her heels on his buttocks.

POSITION 34. TWINING

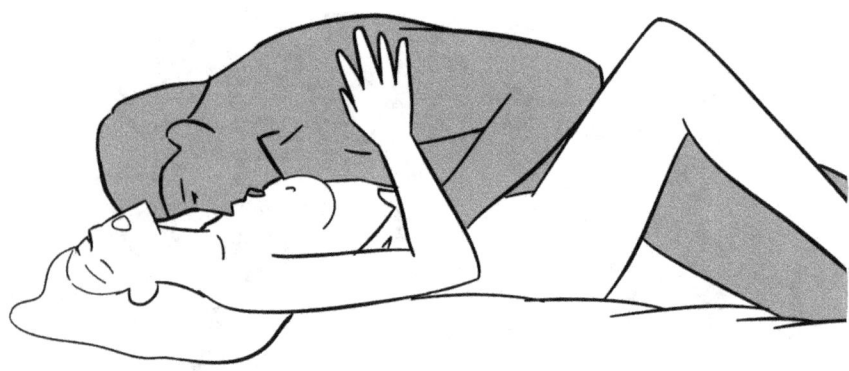

He lies in between her legs. She hooks her legs around the top of his thighs.

POSITION 35. CLASPING

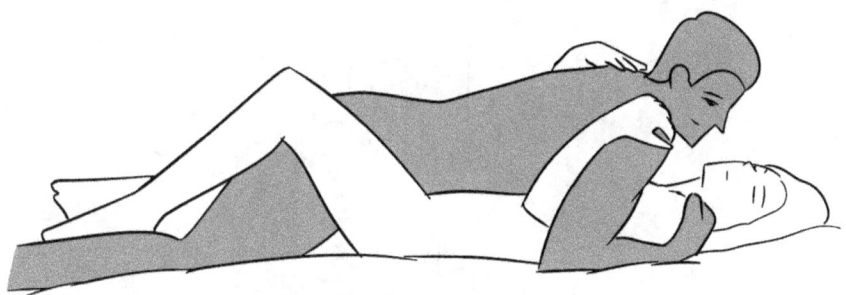

He lies on top, with his legs in between hers. Her feet wrap over his legs and rest on the inside.

POSITION 36. FIXING A NAIL

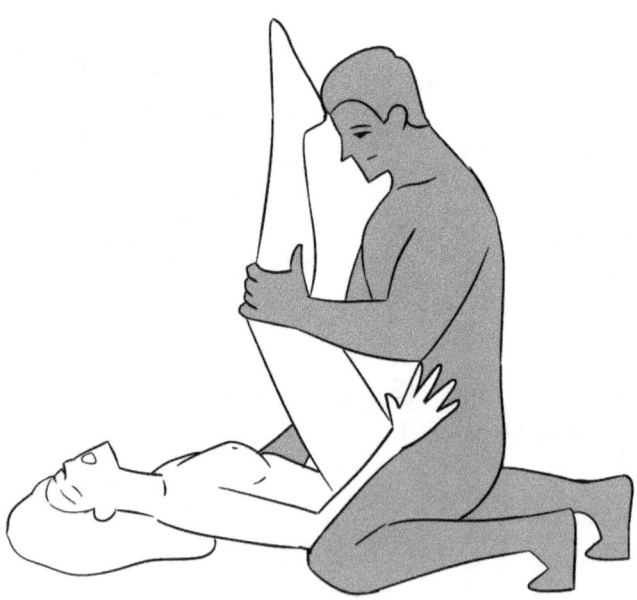

He kneels up close to her. One of her legs is raised, with her heel at his forehead. From there, he can massage her calf and thigh with one hand, while playing with her clitoris or anus with the other. She can vary the sensations by moving her leg.

Related Chapters:

- Massage

POSITION 37. HALF PRESSED

She raises her knees to her chest. He kneels up close to her with his legs spread. One of her legs stretches past his waist and under his arm. Her other foot is placed on his chest. She grabs him by the thighs and he holds her thigh and foot. He should keep his buttocks relaxed and can massage her foot. She can caress his buttocks and thighs and move her hips on him.

Related Chapters:

- Massage

POSITION 38. HORSE SHAKES FEET

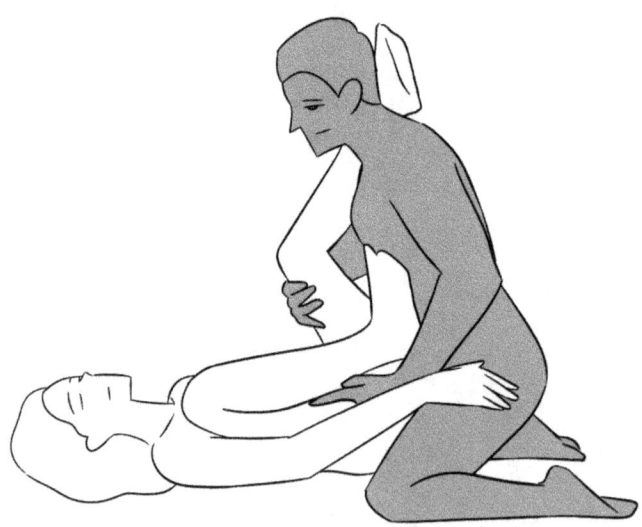

She draws her knees to her chest. He kneels up close, with his knees on either side of her body. One of her legs goes over his shoulder, while her other foot can rest on his stomach or chest. She can shake her raised foot as he thrusts.

POSITION 39. SPLITTING OF BAMBOO

He is up against her on one knee. That knee is on the outside of her torso. His other leg is stretched back. Her leg that is on the same side as his bent knee is on his shoulder. Her other leg wraps around his outstretched leg. She swaps the position of her legs throughout intercourse.

POSITION 40. ANKLE HOLD

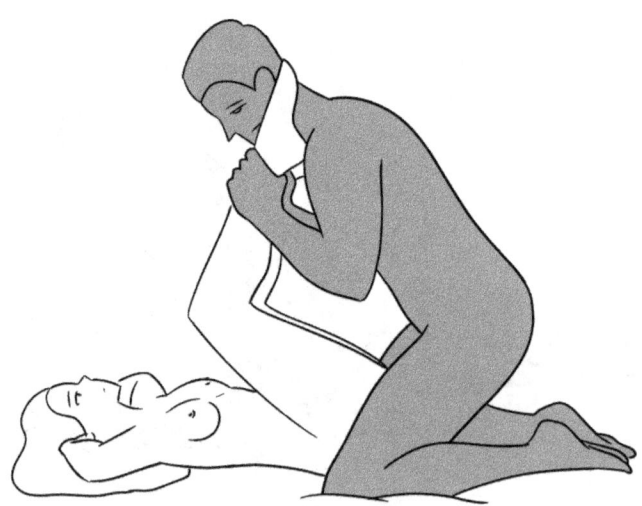

He grabs her by the ankles, with his knees on either side of her buttocks. He holds her feet near his face.

POSITION 41. FETAL FLOWER

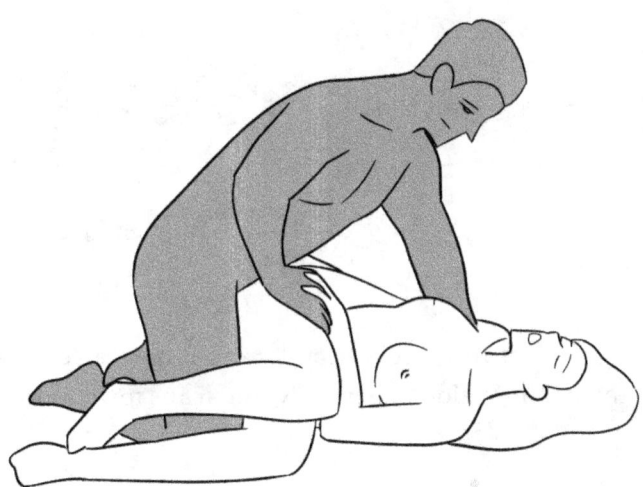

She bends her legs at the knees and leans them to one side. He kneels up against her, behind her legs. She can move her legs in a cyclic motion.

POSITION 42. ENCIRCLING

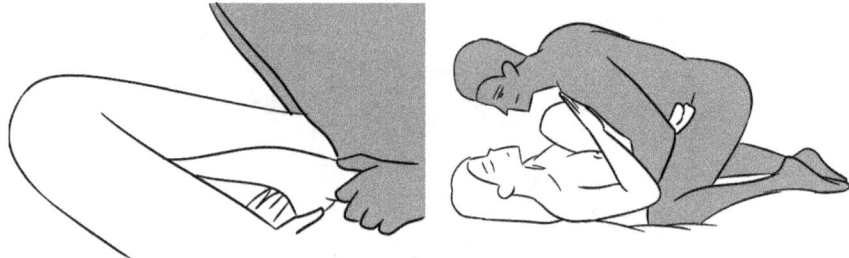

She brings her feet to her chest and crosses her calves. He kneels, with his feet on either side of her body, and leans toward her.

POSITION 43. HELD FEET

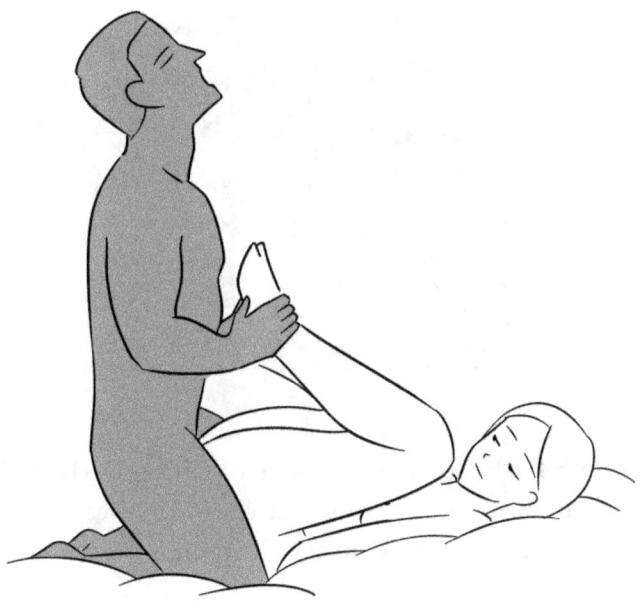

He grabs her by the feet and kneels, with a knee on either side of her. He brings her feet together and pushes her knees to her chest. He can massage her feet.

POSITION 44. HORSE CROSS FEET

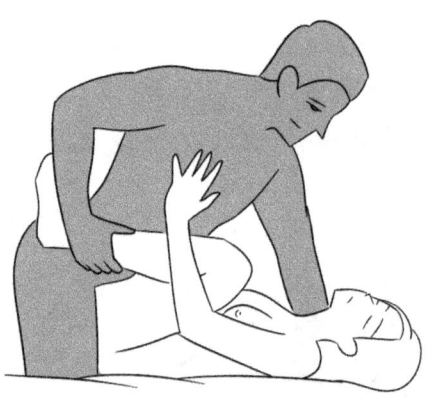

He kneels with his knees on either side of her body. He grabs one of her ankles and pushes her knee to her chest. He uses his other hand to help support himself. As he thrusts, he pumps her leg.

POSITION 45. INTACT POSTURE

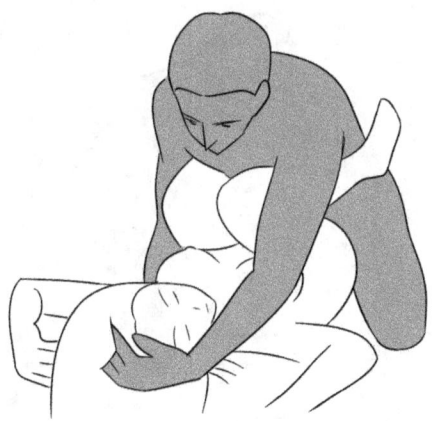

She brings her knees to her chest and keeps them close together. He is on his knees and presses into her, with his chest on her knees. They should start gently.

POSITION 46. JADE JOINT

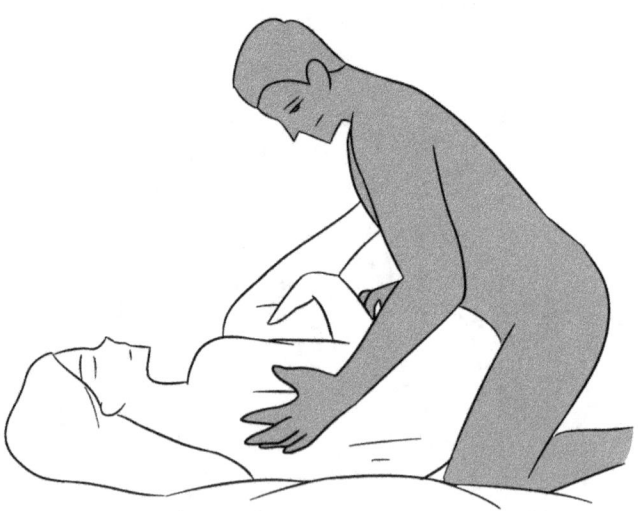

She lies on her side and brings her upper knee to her chest, with her bottom leg straight. She uses her hand to help pull it into position. He kneels with one knee at her back and the other wherever it feels comfortable.

POSITION 47. JOINING THE LOTUS

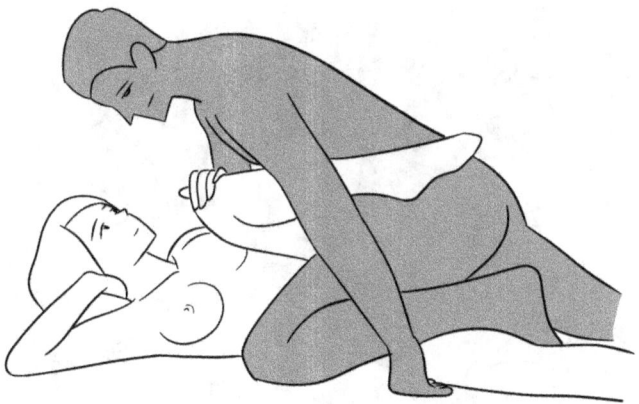

She lies on one side, supporting her head with her hand. She uses her hand to bring her top knee to her chest. Her other leg is laid out flat. He puts his knee between her legs, resting it in front of her body. His foot rests on the thigh of her extended leg. His other leg is stretched out behind him. Her raised calf is between his torso and arm.

POSITION 48. LOTUS

She crosses her ankles and draws her knees up. He kneels with his knees on either side of her and leans over her, resting on his hands. He can lean into her legs if she is flexible enough.

POSITION 49. MANDARIN DUCK

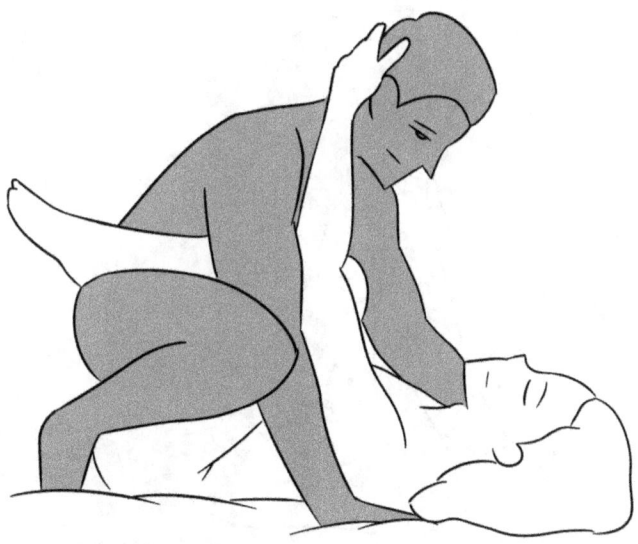

She brings one of her knees to her chest and stretches her other leg out. He squats over her, with his feet on either side of her body. Her raised calf rests on his thigh. He uses his hands to support himself.

POSITION 50. PHOENIX PLAYING IN A RED CAVE

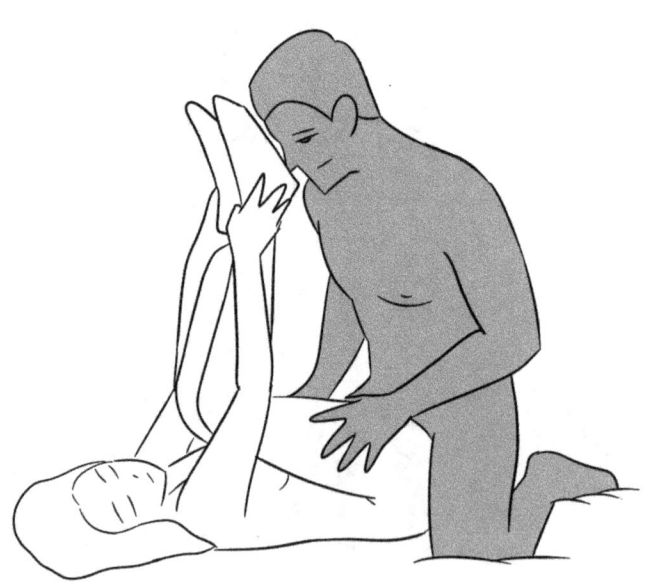

She brings her knees to her chest and holds her ankles together. He kneels with his knees on either side of her.

POSITION 51. PRESSED

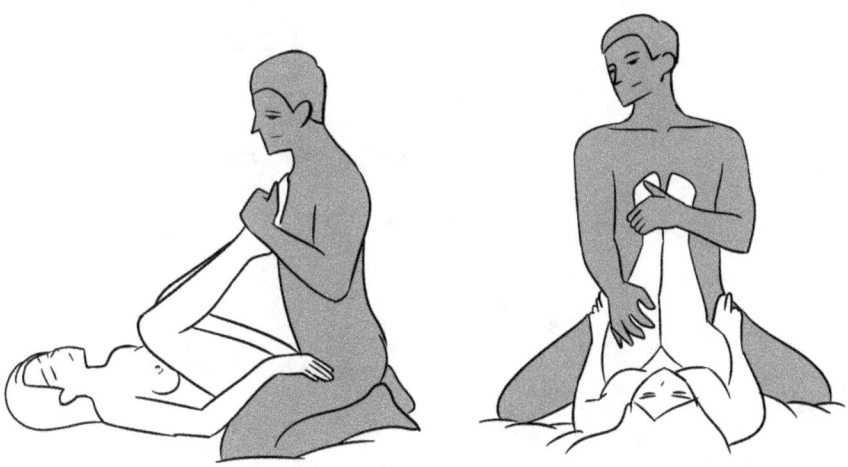

He kneels with his knees on either side of her. She places both her feet on his chest. He massages her feet as he thrusts.

POSITION 52. PUMPING THE WELL

He is in a lunge position. She raises her hips to meet his groin. Her leg, on the same side as his bent leg, is slanted up his torso, so her foot is near his head. He presses his torso against this leg as he thrusts. Her other leg is bent at the knee, with her foot pointing to the sky.

POSITION 53. TURNING

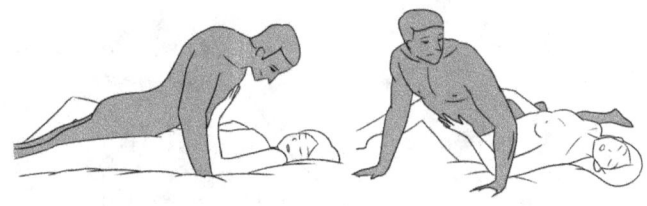

He lies on top of her. Without taking his penis out, he turns 90 degrees, lifting his legs over hers until their bodies are at right angles. She supports his body with her hands to make the turn easier.

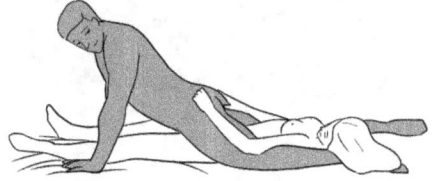

He continues to turn in the same direction until he is facing her feet, with his legs on either side of her body. Using lots of lubrication will make the turn easier.

POSITION 54. RISING

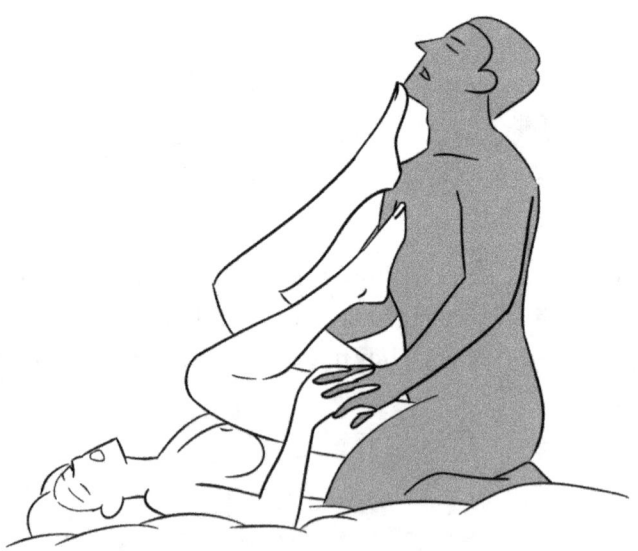

He kneels with his knees on either side of her. She raises her knees towards her chest. One foot is near his shoulder, while the other is on his chest.

POSITION 55. TURTLE MOVE

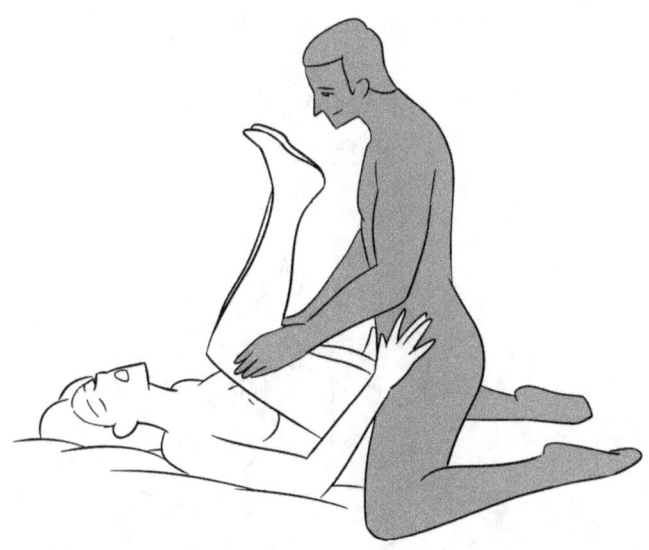

He kneels with his knees on either side of her. She brings her knees to her chest and he keeps her legs together by holding her at her knees. He almost withdraws his penis on every thrust.

POSITION 56. WIFE OF INDRA

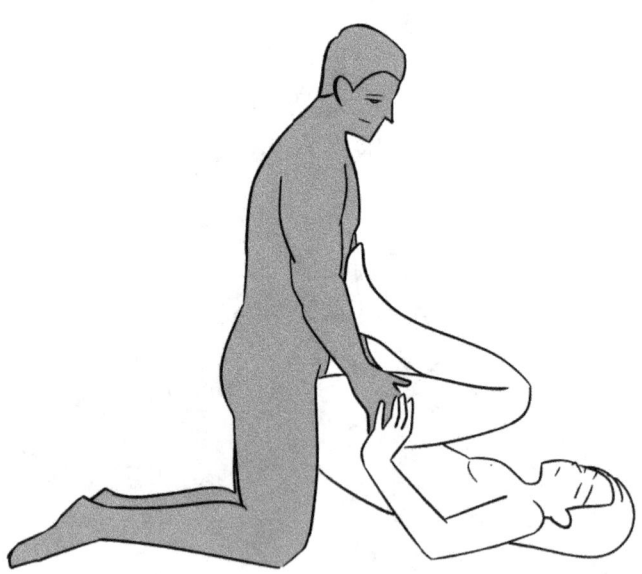

He kneels with his legs close together. She also has her legs together, and raises her hips to meet his groin. Her feet are on his stomach or chest.

WOMAN ON TOP

Positions where the woman is on top enable her to have more control. The man should embrace the submissive feeling.

POSITION 57. BUTTERFLIES IN FLIGHT

She lies on top of him. They are both flat. Her legs are on his legs and her chest is on his chest. They hold hands outstretched to their sides. He flexes his feet and she pushes against them to slide up and down on his body.

She can raise her leg to get more of a push if she needs to.

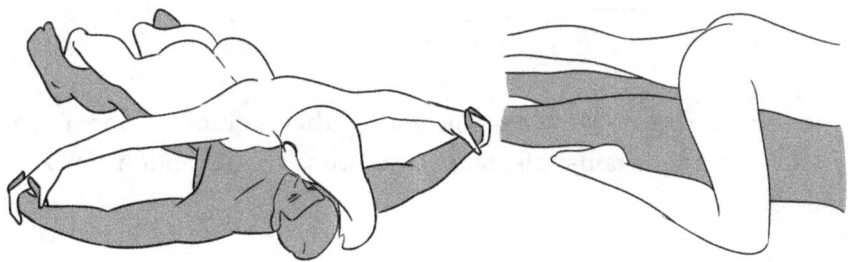

POSITION 58. FISH

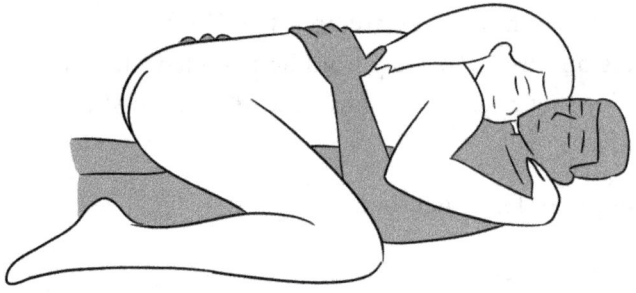

She straddles him, with her knees on either side of his torso. Her chest is pressed against his. She can move vertically and/or horizontally on him.

POSITION 59. INTERCHANGE OF COITION

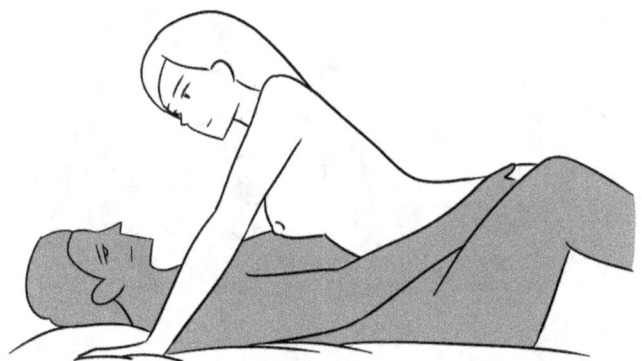

He raises his knees a little and spreads them apart. She lies in between his legs, supporting herself with her hands.

POSITION 60. INVERTED EMBRACE

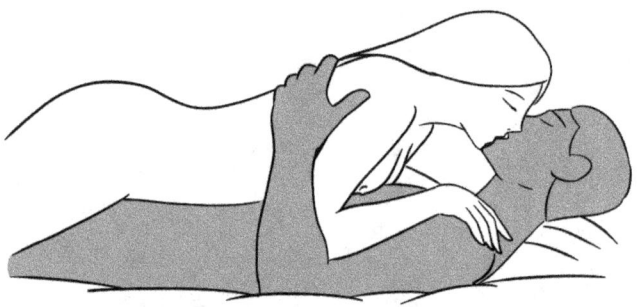

She lies flat on top of him. Their legs are together.

POSITION 61. SHARING REINS

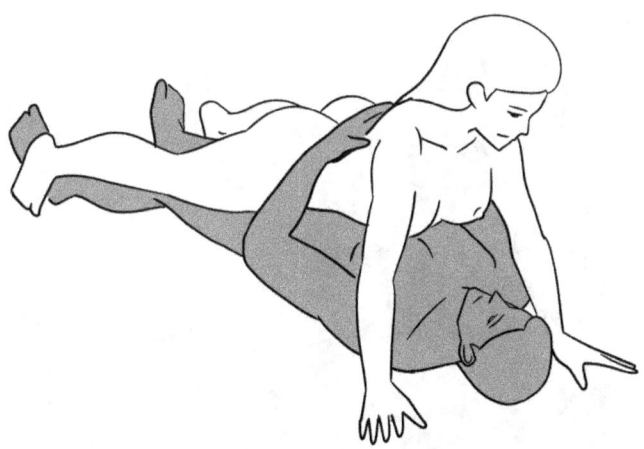

With their legs slightly spread, she lays on top of him. She supports her weight on her hands, which are placed on either side of his head. She pushes to raise her chest off his.

POSITION 62. ACCOMPLISHING POSITION

He sits cross-legged. She sits on him and leans back on one hand. She raises one leg in the air while planting her other foot on the floor.

POSITION 63. ALTERNATIVE MOVEMENT OF PIERCING

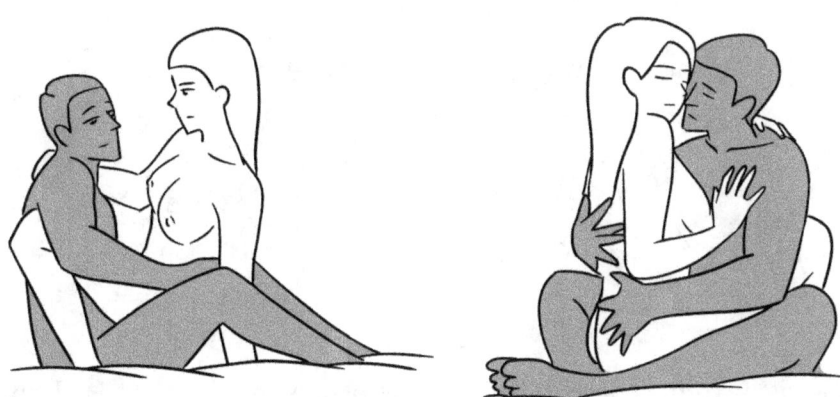

He sits with the soles of his feet together. She sits in between his legs, with her legs on the outside of his hips and her feet planted on the floor. She leans back on one hand and uses the other to grab his shoulder. Alternatively, she can sit close to him with her feet off or on the floor.

POSITION 64. FROG FASHION

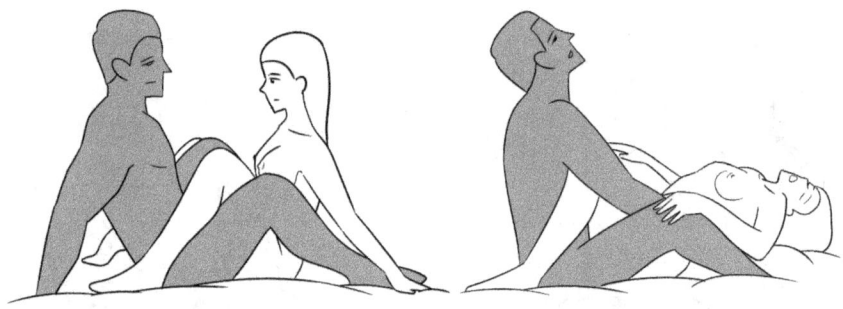

He sits with his knees raised and feet planted on the floor. He leans back onto his hands. She sits in the same position, with one leg in between his legs. Their legs alternate. Their feet are placed on the outside of each other's bodies.

From here, he can hold onto her if she wants to lean back.

POSITION 65. KAMA'S WHEEL

He sits with his legs stretched out. She straddles him, with a leg on either side of him.

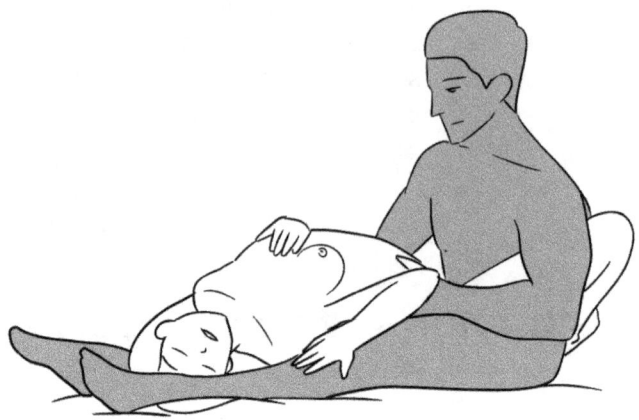

Their upper bodies can be close together or she can lean back.

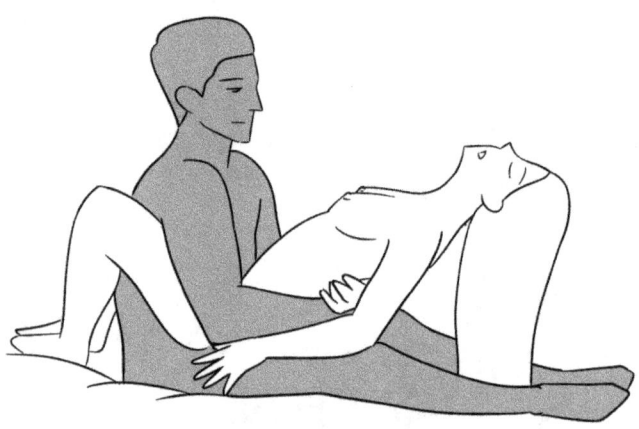

She moves herself up and down or in circles.

POSITION 66. CRYING OUT

He sits with his legs out and she straddles him. Her legs are slung over his arms and he grabs her waist. She can use her hand behind her for support.

POSITION 67. LOTUS INVERTED

He sits crossed-legged. She straddles him, with her feet planted behind him. They hug close and he lifts her up and down on himself. She can also take some weight on her feet. From here, he can lie down while she moves, or she can lean back on her hands and rock back and forth.

POSITION 68. LOVING LIFT

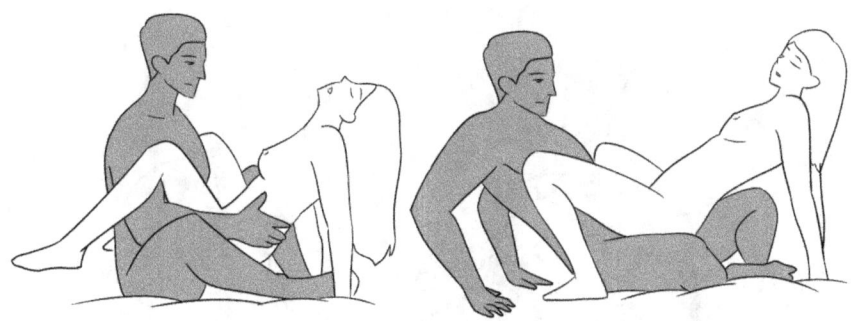

He sits with the soles of his feet together. She sits inside his legs with her feet on either side of his body. Her legs go over his arms at the elbows and he holds her waist. She leans back, supporting her weight on her hands. He closes his thighs slightly to help support her. He moves her on him.

If he gets tired, she can put her feet on the floor and rock on him while he leans back.

POSITION 69. PAIRED FEET

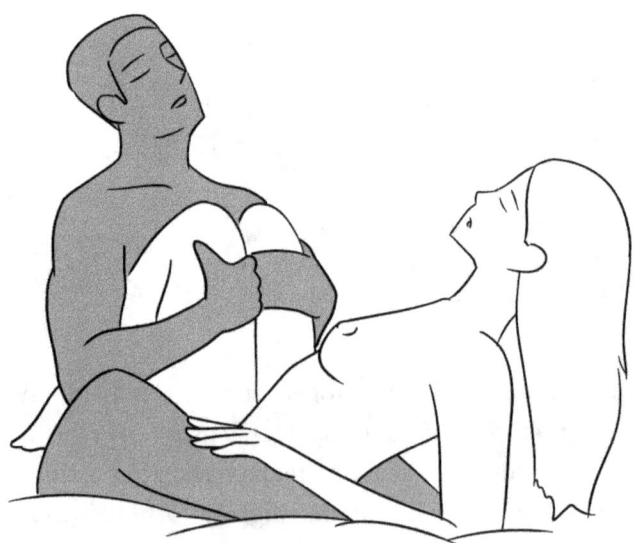

He sits with his legs wide apart. She sits on him, with her feet on either side of him. She leans back and he brings her knees together.

POSITION 70. POSITION OF EQUALS

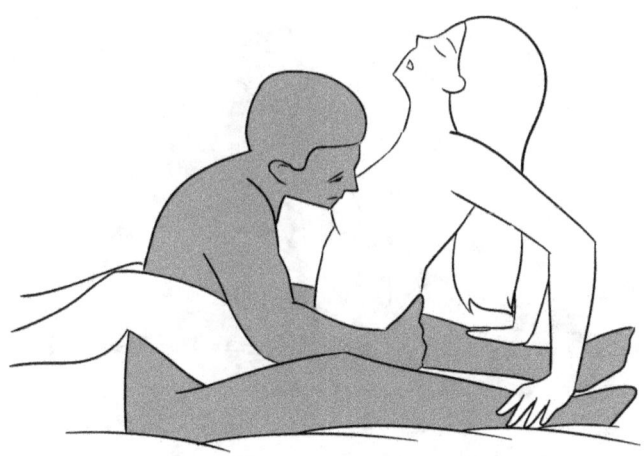

He sits with his legs stretched out in front of him. She sits between his legs with her legs crossed around his torso in the air. She leans back, placing her hands on his ankles.

POSITION 71. SINGING MONKEY

He sits with his legs stretched out in front of him. She sits between his legs, with her legs crossed around his torso and her feet planted on the floor. Their chests are close together. She can lean back on her hand to thrust on him.

POSITION 72. SNAKE TRAP

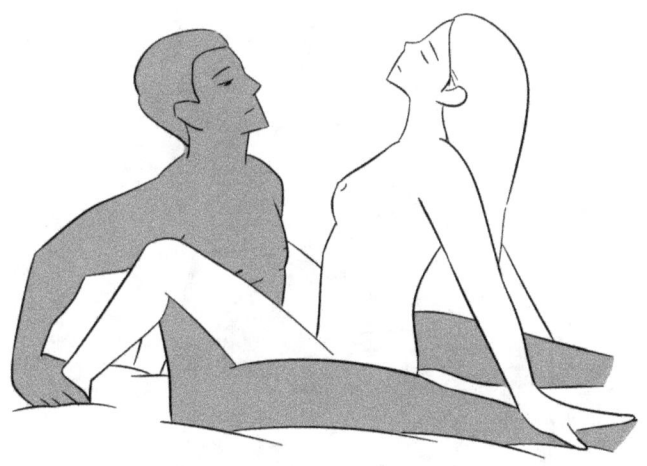

He sits with his legs stretched out in front of him. She sits between his legs, with her legs on either side of his torso and her feet planted on the floor. They both lean back, holding each other's feet for support as they rock.

POSITION 73. YIN AND YANG

This is also known as Yab Yum. He sits cross-legged and she sits on top of him. They hold each other close and she crosses her legs around his back.

POSITION 74. ASCENDING POSITION

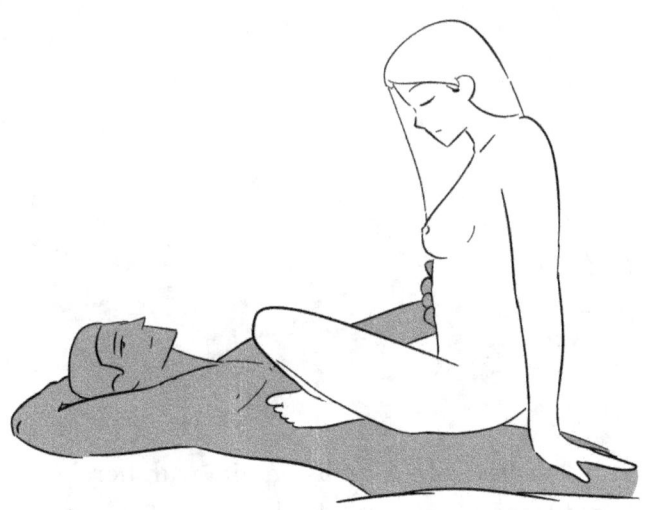

He lies down flat and she sits on him with crossed legs.

POSITION 75. BUTTERFLY

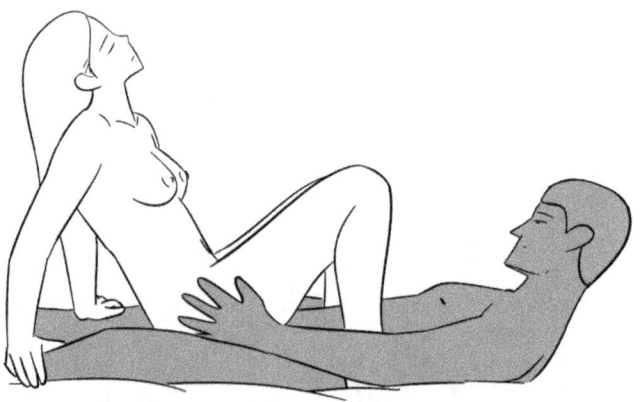

He lies flat on his back and she sits on him with her feet planted on either side of his torso. She leans back and holds his legs. If she gets tired, she can go to her knees.

POSITION 76. CAT AND MOUSE SHARING A HOLE

He lies flat on his back with his legs close together. She lies on top of him with her legs on the outside of his. She supports her weight with her arms.

POSITION 77. CATBIRD SEAT

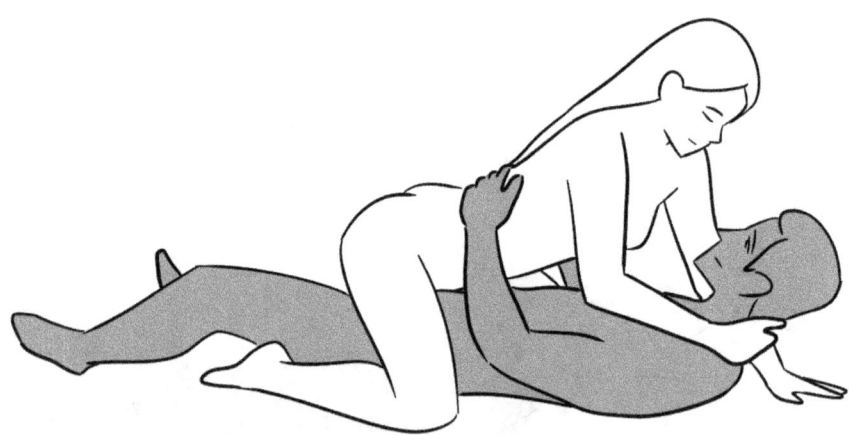

He lies on his back and she kneels over him, a knee on either side of his body. She bends over him so that they are parallel to each other. She can lean forward to get more clitoral stimulation or lean back to hit the G-spot.

POSITION 78. LOVE SEAT

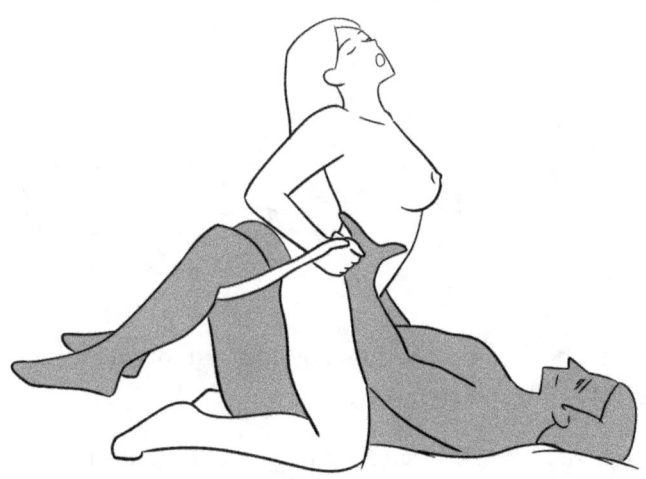

He lies on his back and she sits on top of him, with a knee on either side of his body. He lifts his knees towards her buttocks. She can use some material such as a scarf, to gain more leverage. She can put her feet flat on the floor and lean back into his thighs.

POSITION 79. ORGASMIC ROLE-REVERSAL

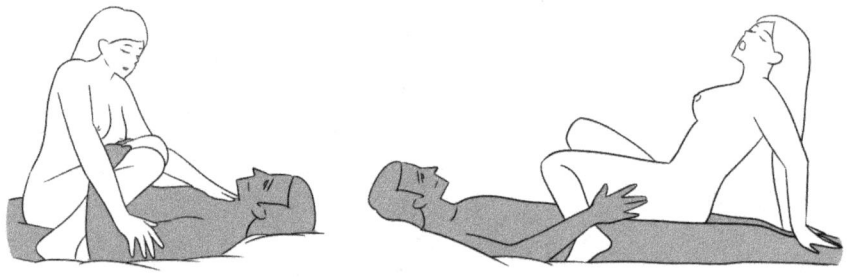

He lies on his back and she squats on him, a foot on either side of his body. He holds her legs together.

For a change of angle, she can lean back and hold his legs.

POSITION 80. PAIR OF TONGS

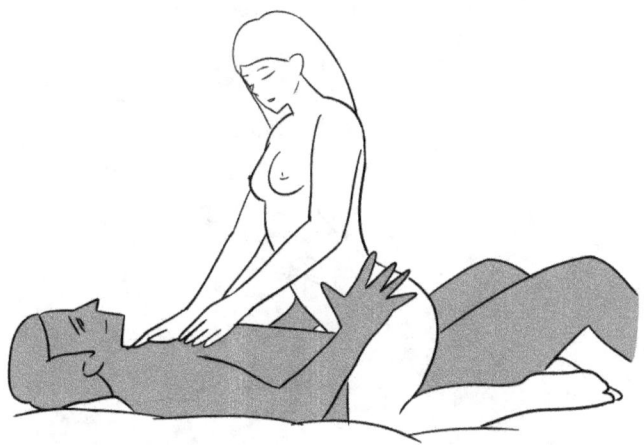

He lies on his back and she sits on top of him, with a knee on either side of his torso. She clasps his hips between her thighs, then slides up and down and forward and backward. She can push his thighs together with her feet.

POSITION 81. RACE OF THE MEMBER

He lies on his back and draws his knees to his chest. She squats on him, with her feet on either side of his buttocks. Her knees are on the outside of his knees. His legs come over her thighs and under her arms.

POSITION 82. HANGING BOW

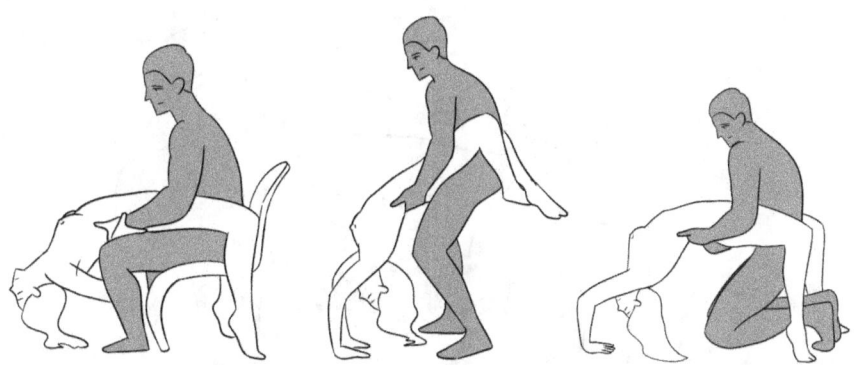

He sits on a chair and she straddles him. He supports her lower back and she grabs his wrists as she arches back. Her legs dangle, relaxed. She then places her hands on the floor and he slowly stands. She crosses her feet behind him.

Finally, he lowers himself down to his knees. Her feet may touch the floor.

POSITION 83. SPIDER

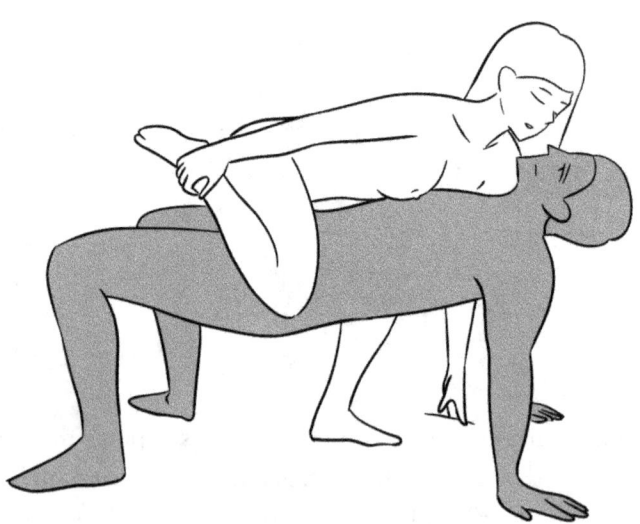

He raises himself on his hands and feet, facing the ceiling. She straddles him, keeping at least one foot planted firmly on the floor.

POSITION 84. GOAT AND THE TREE

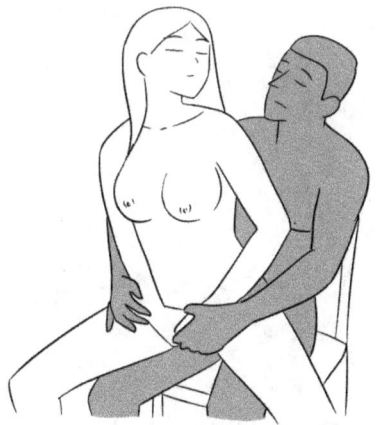

He sits on a chair and she sits on top of him, facing away from him.

POSITION 85. MARE

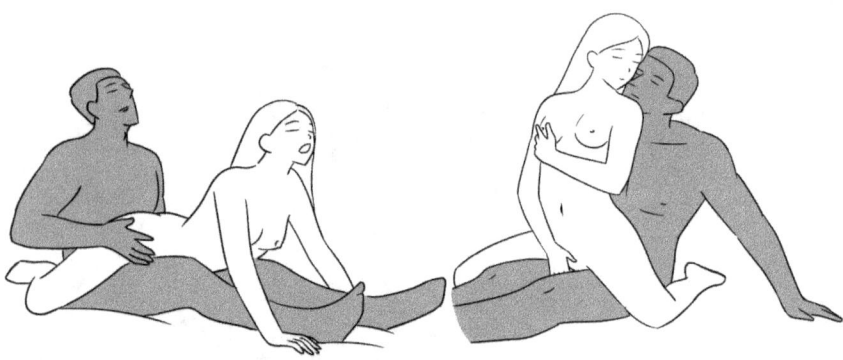

He sits with his legs stretched out in front of him. She faces away from him and sits on him. Her knees are on either side of his hips, with her feet behind him. She bends forward and supports herself on her hands, which are on either side of his feet. She uses her vaginal muscles to milk his penis.

She can sit up straight and stimulate her clitoris.

POSITION 86. RABBIT GROOMING

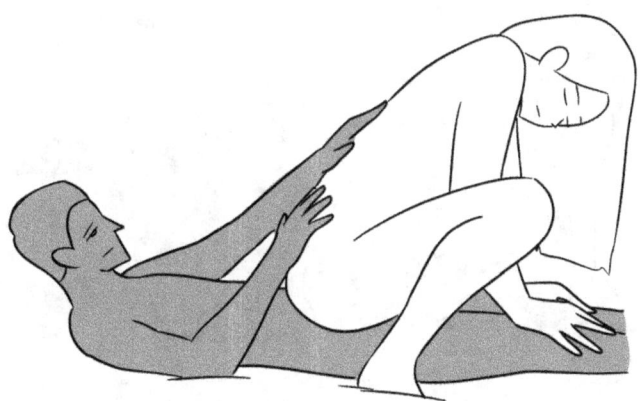

He lies on his back and she squats onto him with her legs on the outside of his legs, facing away from him. If she gets tired, she can switch to a kneeling position.

POSITION 87. RECIPROCAL SIGHTS OF THE POSTERIORS

He lies on his back and she squats onto him with her legs between his. She is facing away from him. She can lean forward for an erotic view.

POSITION 88. REVERSE CRAB

He lies on his back and she sits on him, facing away from him. Her feet are on either side of his legs. She leans back on her hands, which are planted on either side of him.

POSITION 89. SWING

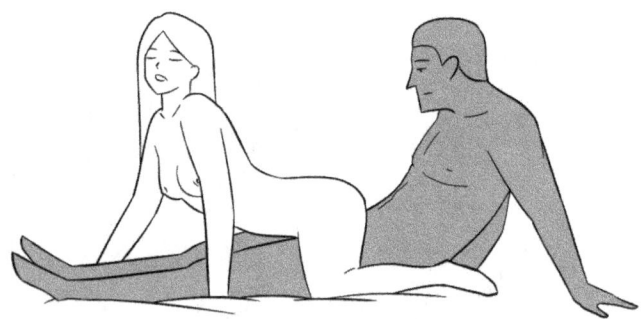

He sits with his legs stretched out in front of him and leans back onto his hands. Facing away from him, she gets on her hands and knees, which are placed on the outside of his legs. He can run his fingers down her spine while she moves on him.

POSITION 90. SPINNING THE TOP

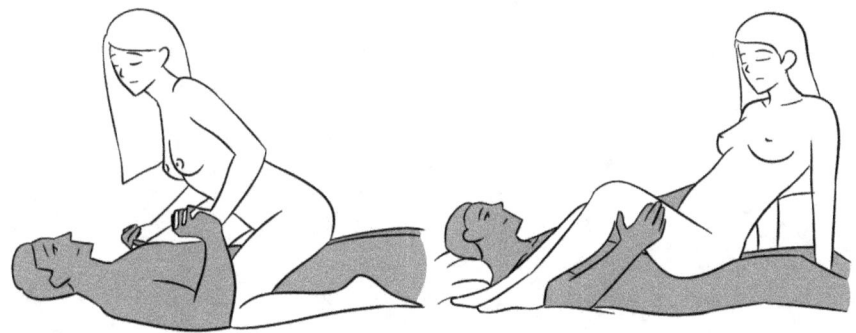

He lies on his back with his legs stretched out in front of him. She straddles him, with her knees on either side of his body. She leans back onto her hands, bringing her feet to the outside of one of his shoulders. They clasp hands for support, and she arches her back. When ready, she continues to spin on him, using her hands to support some of her weight.

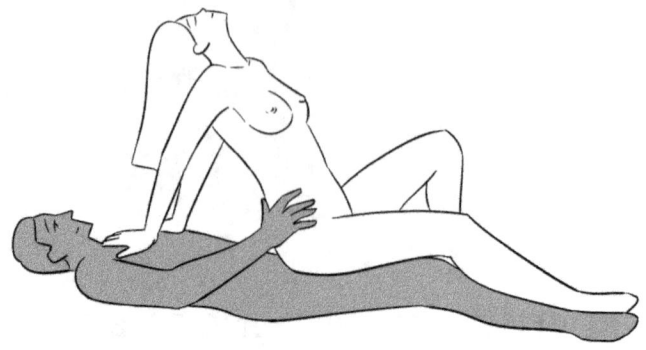

She ends up facing away from him, leaning back on her hands, which are placed on his chest. She leans forwards and backwards to experience different sensations.

POSITION 91. TOPPING AND TURNING

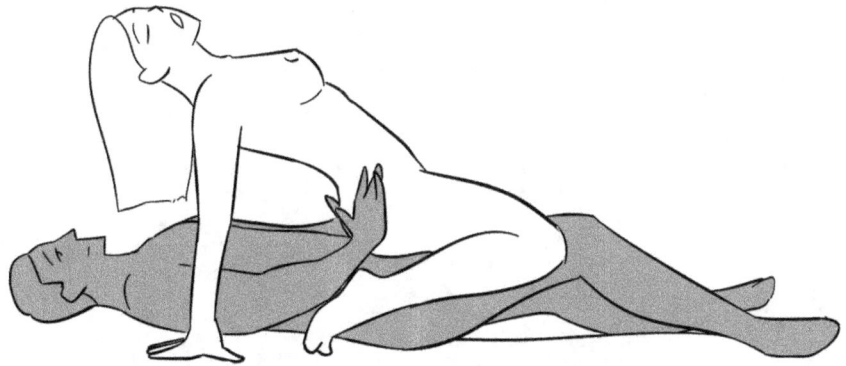

He lies on his back. Facing away from him, she squats on him, with her feet on the outside of his legs. She then leans back onto her hands, which are placed on either side of his shoulders.

FROM BEHIND

Although not as intimate as positions where they are facing each other, a man taking his lover from behind can give great pleasure. It is a highly dominant position for the man.

POSITION 92. 6TH POSTURE (DOGGY STYLE)

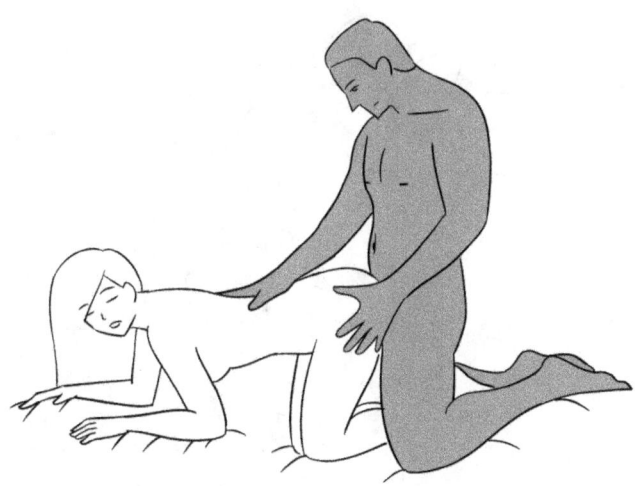

She gets on her hands (or forearms) and knees. He gets on his knees behind her. His knees are on the outside of her legs.

POSITION 93. LOVING CHAIR

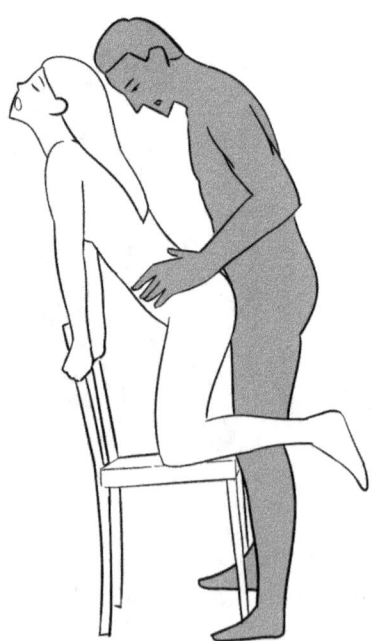

She kneels on a chair facing, the back of it and holds the back for support. He stands behind her.

POSITION 94. RISING PILLOWS

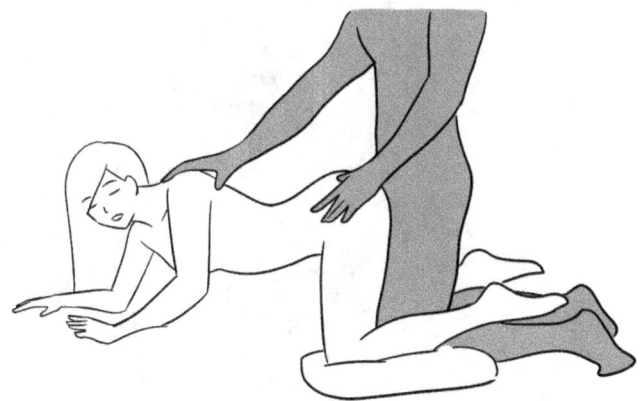

She gets on her knees and relaxes over a mound of pillows that raises her buttocks into the air. Her legs are spread, and he kneels in between them.

POSITION 95. STANDING DOGGY

She gets on her knees in an upright position and spreads her legs a little. He kneels with his knees in between hers. His chest is pressed to her back.

POSITION 96. TIGER STEP

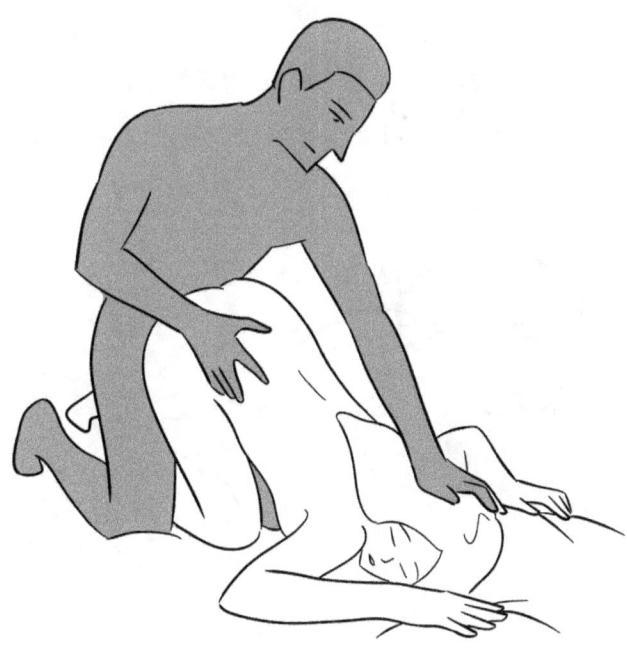

She gets on her knees with her feet crossed and leans forwards, relaxing her head, arms and chest on the floor. Her bum is in the air. He kneels behind her, with his knees on either side of hers.

POSITION 97. WHITE TIGER

She rests on one knee and her elbows. He kneels with one knee on either side of her grounded knee. He holds her other leg up on the outside of his thigh. She can hook her raised leg around his buttocks.

POSITION 98. CICADA ON A BOUGH

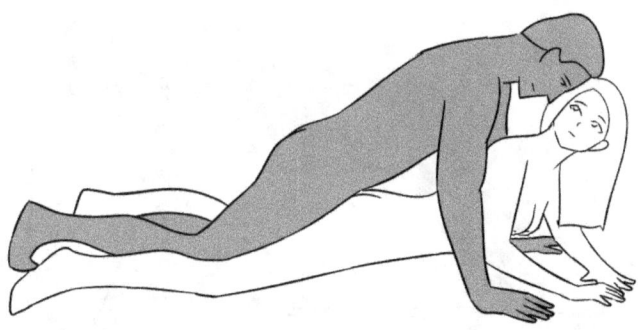

She lies on her stomach, with her legs spread. He lies on top of her, with his legs in between hers. He supports himself on his hands. She can do the same.

POSITION 99. COITUS FROM BEHIND

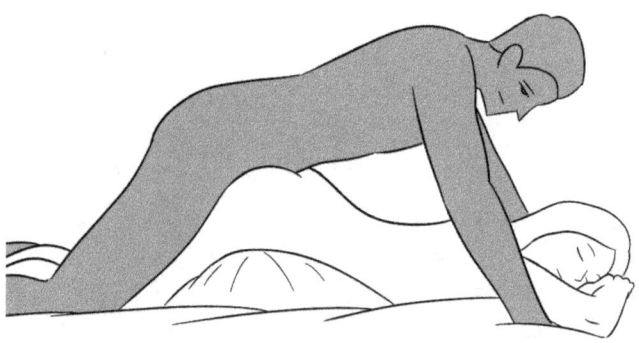

She lies on her stomach, with her legs together and with a cushion under her pelvis to raise her buttocks. He lies on top of her with his legs on either side of hers. He supports himself with his hands on either side of her shoulders.

POSITION 100. ELEPHANT

She lies on her stomach. He lies on top of her, raising his chest by pushing his hands into the floor on either side of her waist.

POSITION 101. CONGRESS OF A COW

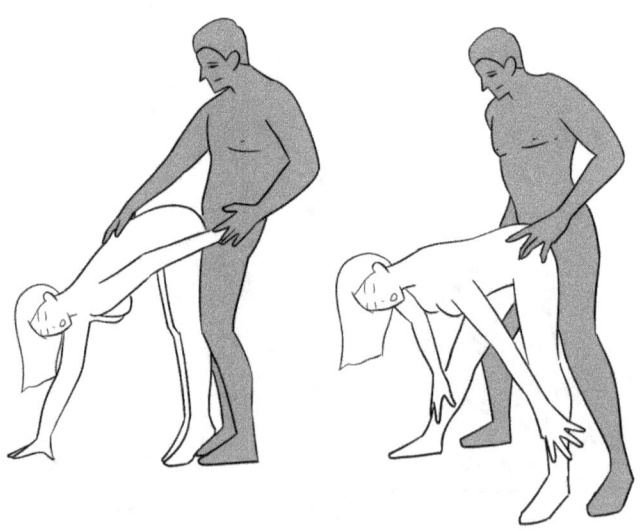

From a standing position, she bends over, placing one or both hands on the floor. Her legs stay straight. He stands behind her and pulls her back and forth onto him. If she is not that flexible, she can put her hands on a raised object such as a chair or the bed. Her legs can be together or apart.

POSITION 102. THE 'QUICKIE'

Although many positions can accommodate the quickie, coming from behind while standing often works the best. Clothes do not even have to be removed, and the man has complete control over his climax.

Note: Quickies are a lot of fun, but don't get addicted, otherwise you'll miss a lot of pleasure.

POSITION 103. FREESTANDING LOVE

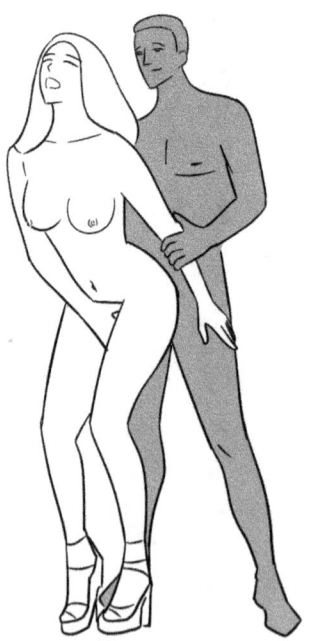

She stands with her legs together and squats just a little. He stands behind her.

POSITION 104. LATE SPRING DONKEY

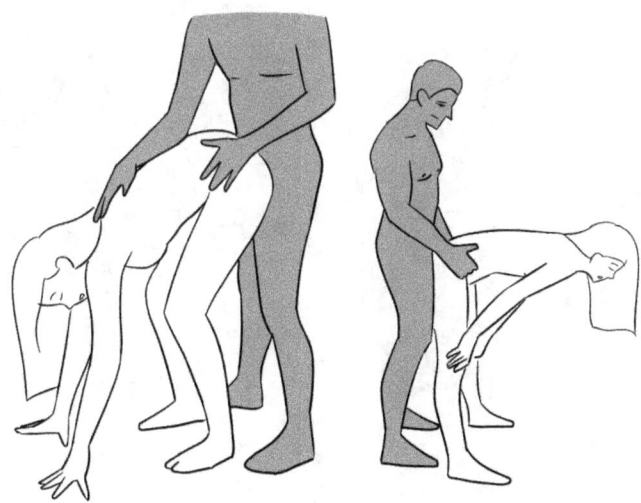

She stands with her legs apart and places both hands on the floor, bending her knees a little. He stands behind her. If she wants, she can straighten her legs and place her hands on her knees.

POSITION 105. 9TH POSTURE

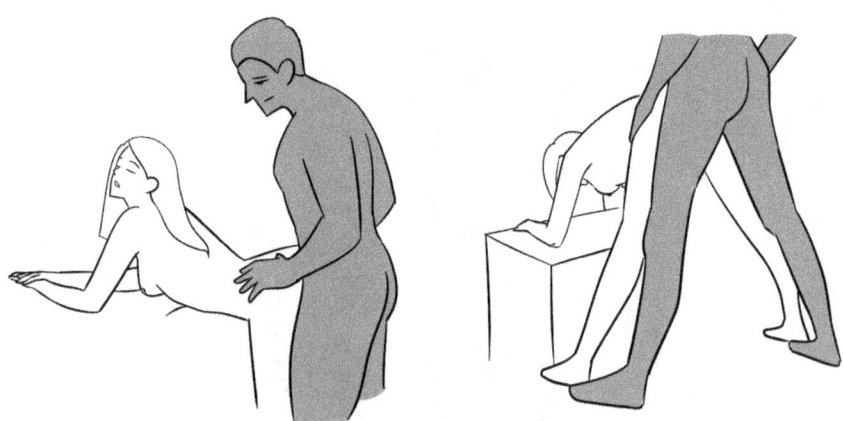

She kneels, facing the edge of the bed or another piece of furniture, and rests her upper body on it. She uses her forearms to prop herself up. He kneels behind her. Alternatively, they can stand.

POSITION 106. LOVING GAZE

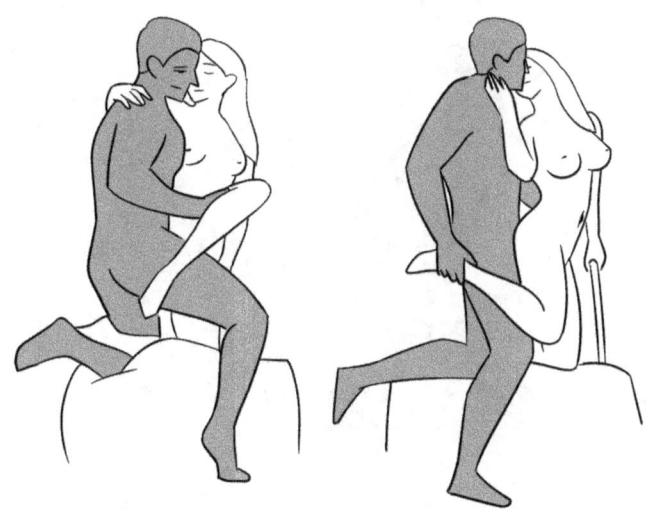

She kneels on the edge of the bed. He comes up behind her, placing one knee on the bed and one foot on the floor. He grabs the leg or foot of hers closest to the edge, and holds it on the outside of the leg on which he is standing. She turns to look at him, which aligns their groins.

POSITION 107. STANDING SPONTANEITY

He comes up behind her. She bends over on any available surface.

STANDING POSITIONS

Some standing positions can be difficult to achieve, as they require more flexibility and/or strength.

POSITION 108. BAMBOO

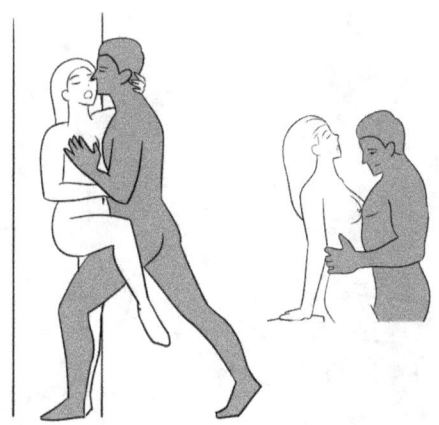

Her back is to a wall and he lunges to her so their chests are close together. She puts her leg over his forward-most leg.

If she is up against something lower (such as a bed or table), she can lean back on her hands while he grabs her around the waist.

POSITION 109. BELLY TO BELLY

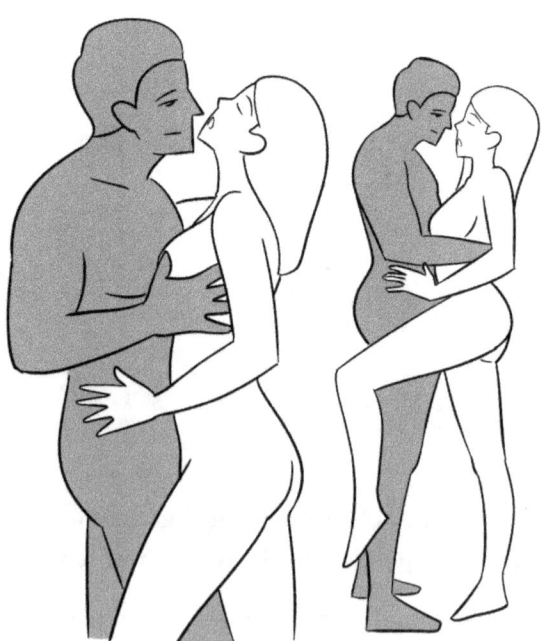

They stand face to face, close against each other. She can hook a leg over his thigh. It will help if she thrusts her pelvis forward.

POSITION 110. DRIVING THE PEG HOME

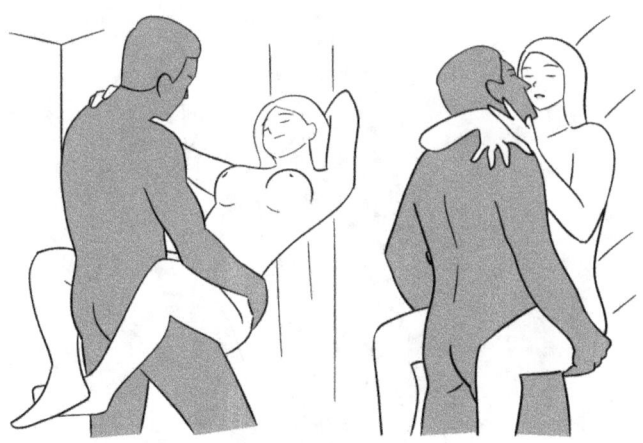

He stands. She wraps her legs around his waist while holding his shoulders. She can lean back into a wall or be pressed tightly against it.

POSITION 111. STANDING SPLIT

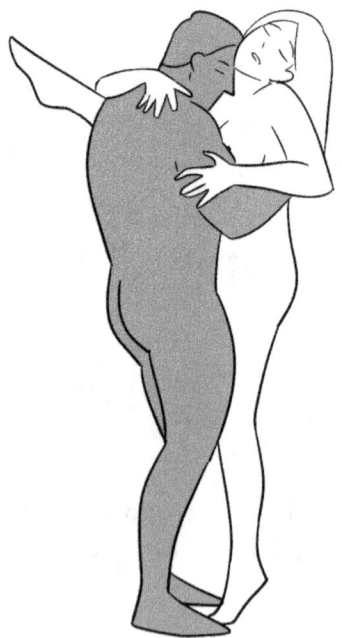

They are both standing, facing each other. She lifts one leg high over his shoulder.

POSITION 112. SUPPORTED CONGRESS

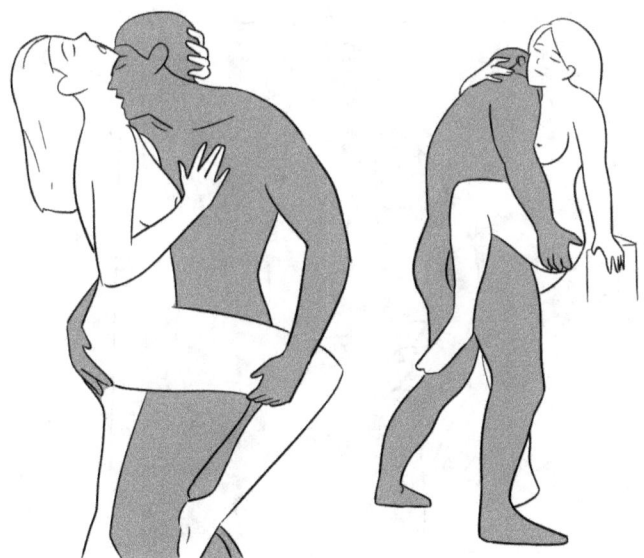

They stand facing each other, with their legs alternating. She lifts one leg and he uses his hand to support it. This position can be free standing or adopted with her backed up against something.

POSITION 113. SUSPENDED CONGRESS

He stands, leaning back against a wall with his legs apart and slightly bent. She sits on him, dangling her legs over his thighs.

POSITION 114. WEEPING WILLOW

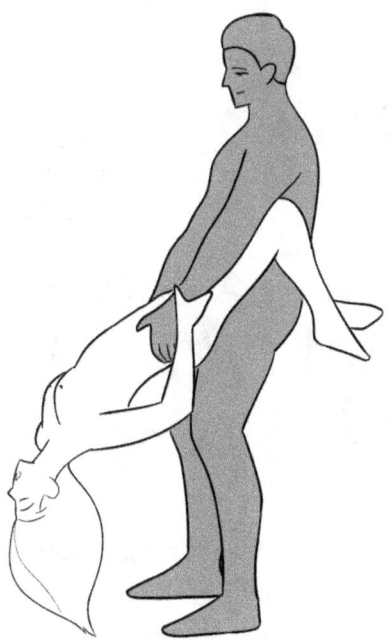

He stands. She wraps her legs around his waist and leans back so her head is near the floor. If he gets tired, he can take a seat.

POSITION 115. WHEELBARROW

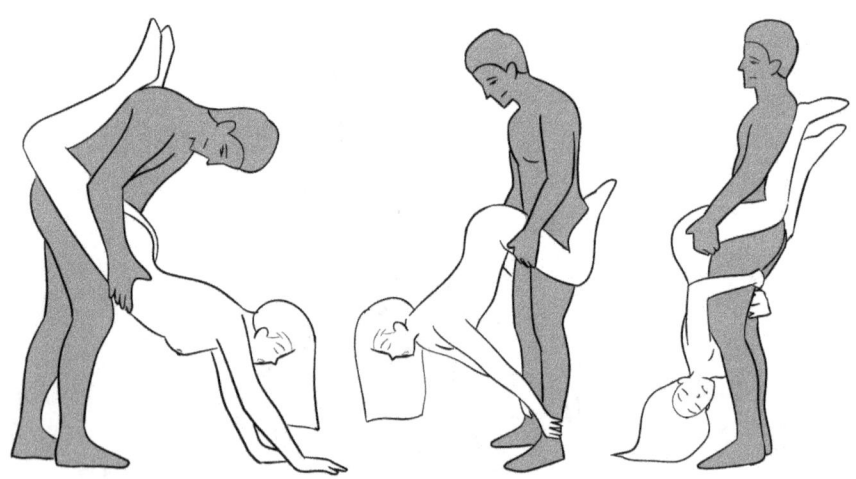

He stands and she stands in front of him, facing away from him. Her hands are on the floor or holding his legs or ankles. Her legs extend past his torso, one leg on each side of him. She can hold onto him with her thighs, wrapping her feet around his waist or on his shoulders.

SIDE ON POSITIONS

Side positions are great for relaxed sex. If you are sleepy or when your body is otherwise not up to other positions, side by side is the answer. It is also highly intimate, and with the often-slow nature of the intercourse, the man can usually last much longer.

POSITION 116. TRANSVERSE LUTE

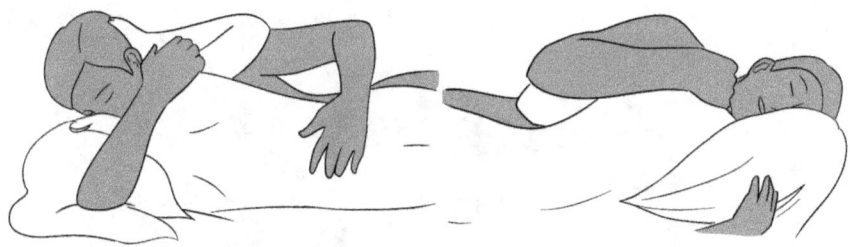

They are both on their sides, facing each other.

They hold each other close, and he slides up and down her body.

POSITION 117. CICADA TO THE SIDE

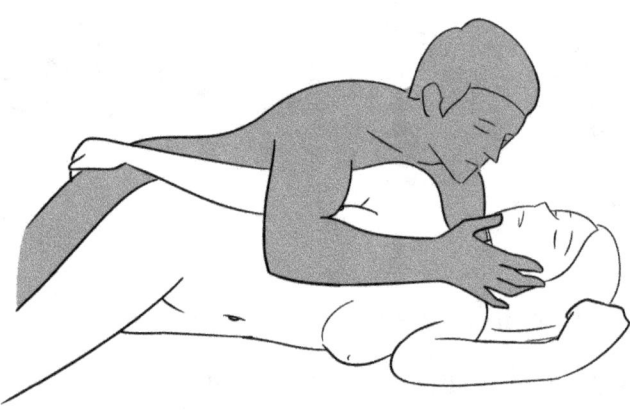

They are both on their sides. She faces away from him. She looks back to him.

POSITION 118. MANDARIN DUCKS

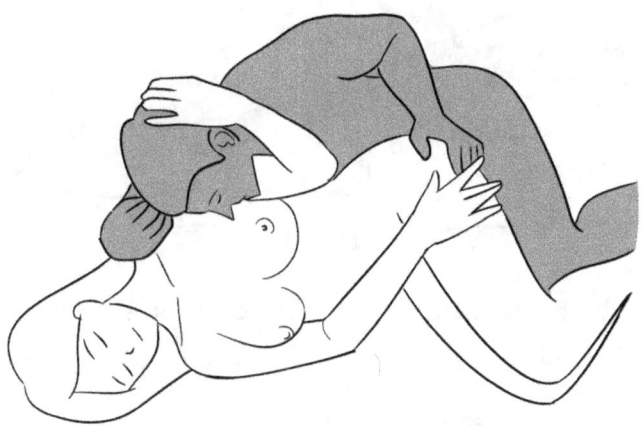

They are both on their sides. She faces away from him. Their legs are bent, and his knees fit behind hers. She can allow for deeper penetration by bringing her knees to her chest.

POSITION 119. TWO FISHES

They are both on their sides facing each other, with their legs stretched out.

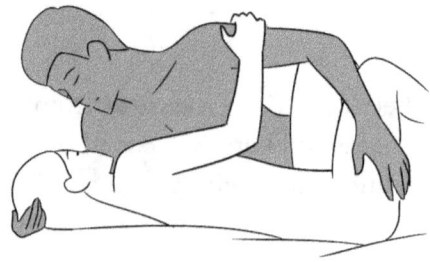

Once he is inside her, she places her legs on top of his.

POSITION 120. 5TH POSTURE

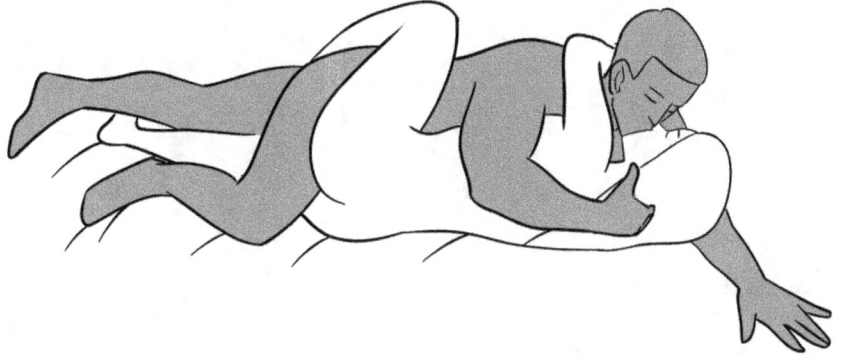

They both lie on their sides, facing each other. His top leg is in between her legs, and they hold each other close. She rests her top leg on his. She can raise her leg higher on his body to allow for deeper penetration.

MISCELLANEOUS POSITIONS

POSITION 121. AUTUMN DOG

She takes a standing position, keeping her legs straight and placing her head and forearms on the floor. He backs up to her, with his feet on either side of hers, until their bums are touching. He keeps his legs fairly straight and touches the floor. He uses his hand to guide his penis inside her, then places it back onto the floor.

POSITION 122. FITTER-IN

They are both sitting upright, with their groins together. One of her legs is on top of his and the other is underneath his. From here, they can lean back onto their hands or lie back completely.

POSITION 123. DRAWING THE BOW

She lies on her side and raises her top leg high in the air. He lies on her bottom leg so they make a plus sign. He faces her back.

They hold each other's legs with their hands.

POSITION 124. SCISSORS

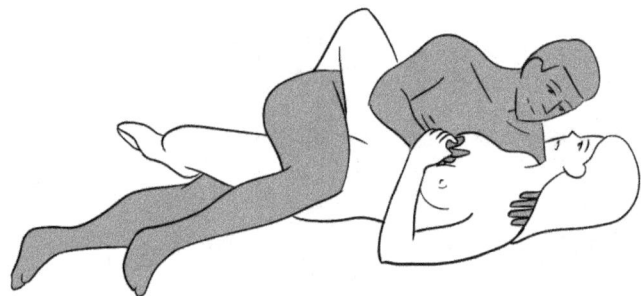

She lies on her side and he lies next to her, facing her back. His bottom leg is under her bottom leg, and his top leg is hooked over her bottom leg. She raises her top leg and turns onto her back to face him, hooking the leg over his waist.

POSITION 125. SITTING ON TOP OF THE WORLD

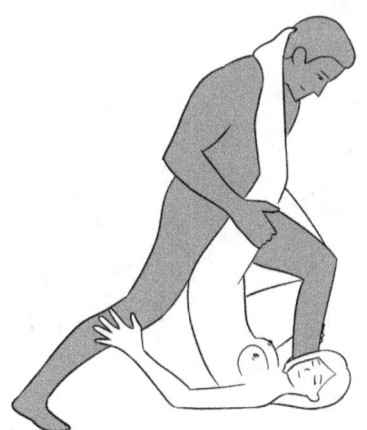

She lies on her back and lifts her legs high in the air, lifting her lower back off the floor. He steps through her legs so one foot is near her head and the other is behind her. One of her legs is angled in between his legs and up his torso, so her foot is near his shoulder.

POSITION 126. SEAGULLS ON THE WING

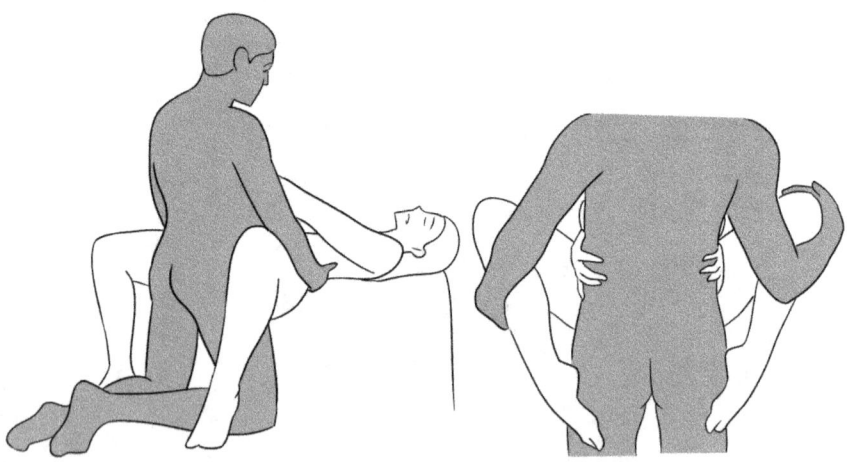

She sits on the edge of a bed (or something similar) with her legs dangling over the edge. She lies back and spreads her legs. He kneels in front of her, between her legs.

She can hook her feet on his buttocks or around his waist.

BONUS - ORAL POSITIONS

These oral position were not part of the original version, so I added them as a bonus instead of retitling the entire book.

ALL FOR HER

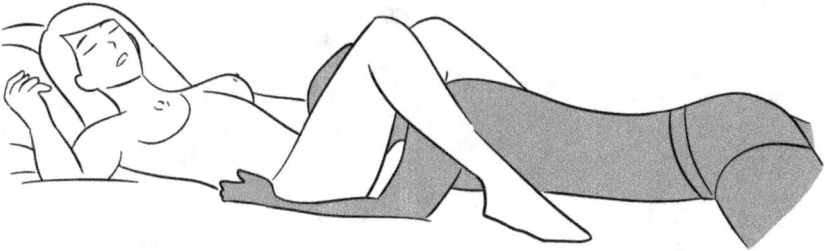

She lies on her back, with her legs spread and feet planted flat. He lies on his stomach, with his head between her legs at her groin.

LEAN BACK

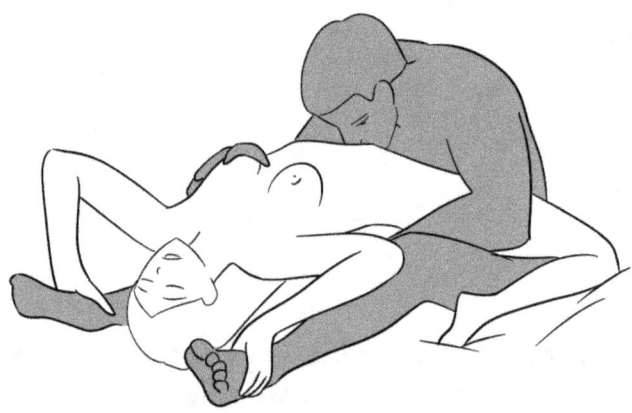

He sits with his legs stretched out in front of him. She kneels astride him, with one knee on either side of his body. She leans back and thrusts her hips up. He bends forward at his torso to meet her groin with his mouth.

RIDING HIS FACE

He lies on his back, with his feet planted on the floor. Facing towards his head, she kneels with one knee on either side of his head and sits on his face.

SIDEWAYS 69

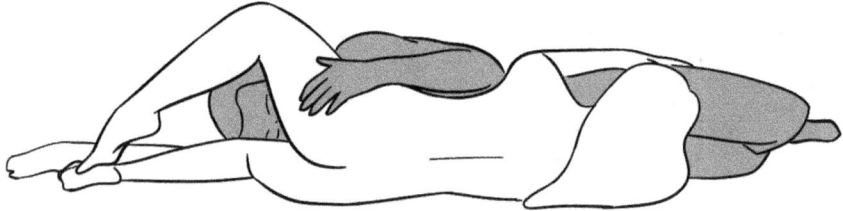

They both lie on their sides, facing each other. They are inverted, so that their mouths are at each other's groins.

69 HER ON TOP

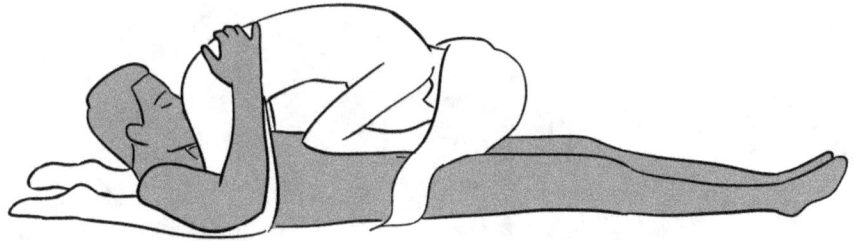

He lies flat on his back. Facing towards his feet, she kneels over him, placing her knees on either side of his upper torso. She bends to meet his groin and he raises his head to meet hers.

69 HIM ON TOP

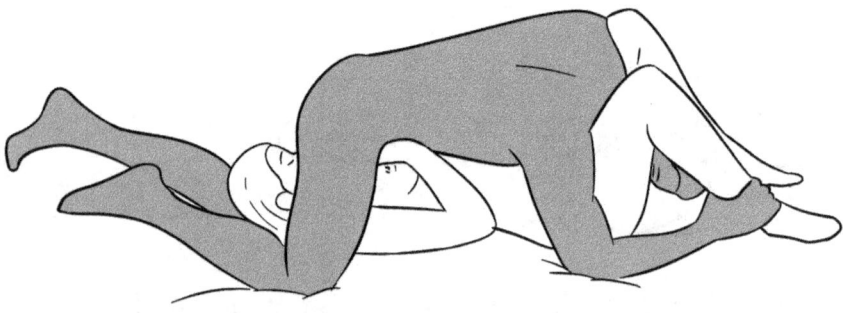

She lies on her back, with her feet on the floor and her legs spread. He faces her feet and kneels, placing his knees on either side of her head. Their heads are in between each other's legs.

STANDING 69

He stands. Her groin is at his mouth, and her legs are wrapped around his head/neck. He helps to hold her up with his hands on her buttocks. Her mouth is on his groin.

LEARN TANTRIC SEX

UNDERSTANDING TANTRIC SEX

Tantra is a spiritual practice in which connection and the full experience of sex is valued over orgasm. Practitioners combine sexual energy to enhance the connection between them and the universe. With tantric sex, you can expect longer sexual interaction and whole-body experiences.

When practicing tantra, do it in a space conducive to meditation (see Your Tantric Space). Stay present and pay attention to the feelings in your body, your breathing, and the movement of your and your lover's energy rising up through the body and into the universe. Build sexual excitement, and then move the sexual energy around. Don't get lost in the moment as you would during normal intercourse. When you climax, if you are in full awareness of the state and stay there for as long as possible, you can bring yourself to a state of enlightenment.

Tantra is meant to be fun and playful. Some concepts and meditations may be a bit too much for some, but lower your inhibitions and you will discover sexual bliss and a focused spirit. Allow the pleasure to come to you, as opposed to striving for it.

Although the focus of this book is on tantric sex, there are a few non-tantric sex exercises. This is because you first need to be in tune with yourself and your partner as sexual beings on a basic level before moving on to tantric sex. It is, of course, highly possible that since you are reading a book about tantric sex that you are already in tune with your sexual being. Just do whatever you wish to do.

At first, you may feel some of these meditations are too "out there." Experiment with what you are comfortable with. After a time, you may wish to try others. Do what you want, when you want, for however long you want, and have fun doing it.

Some of these meditations can only be done with a partner (preferably a lover), but many of them can be adapted to solo meditation. If you do not have a current lover, or your lover is not open to tantra, try searching online for tantra partners.

Creating a Deeper Connection

When you practice tantra, you will connect with the universe in a way most people never imagine. When you practice tantra with your lover, the connection between you will become deeper than ever. When you practice tantra through sex, you will experience the deepest possible physical pleasure.

Some ways to make this connection are:

- Listening to each other with unconditional acceptance and without trying to solve the problem.
- Showing daily physical affection without the expectation of sex.
- Making love with full consciousness.
- Practicing partnered yoga.
- Practicing the many tantric exercises outlined in this publication together.

Being the Witness

While practicing tantra, whether meditative or during sex, observe what you are doing while you are doing it. If you get distracted or anxious, notice these thoughts, then refocus on your breath and the physical sensations in your body.

Related Chapters:

- Your Tantric Space
- Breathing

THE MINDSET OF AN AMAZING SEXUAL BEING

Believe you are an erotic sexual being.

Sex is pleasure. It heals and is healthy.

Have an open mind and be open to your lover.

Release your inhibitions and discover what truly makes you feel good.

Devote your whole self, mind and body, to the moment. Give your all to your lover and receive all that you can.

Feel your whole body, as opposed to just focusing on orgasm.

There's nothing wrong with having a lot of sex. The only way you can have too much sex is if it affects your life in a negative way, such that you neglect work or family, for example.

YOUR TANTRIC SPACE

You will get the most out of your tantric practices if you have a special space that can accumulate the energy.

This space need not be exclusively for tantric practice, but it should be conducive to the practice. Most, if not all, of your tantric practices should be performed in this space.

Fortunately, a tantric space is very conducive to other activities of a similar spiritual/healing/calming nature, such as massage, meditation, yoga, or sleeping. Many people use their bedroom.

The basic principle is to create the right mood by stimulating the senses, and to have everything you will need within easy reach so as to not disturb the mood.

Here are some examples:

- Make a tidy area with soft pillows and comfortable bed sheets (silk, velvet, satin, cotton, etc.).
- Have fresh flowers and incense (jasmine or musk).
- Light candles and/or use dimmed lights.
- Put on some tranquil or sensual music.
- Have mirrors, toys, feathers, silk scarves, and massage oil nearby.
- Have things to pleasure the taste buds, such as honey, chocolate, or grapes.

Related Chapters:

- Massage

CHAKRAS

Chakras are the energy centers in your body. Ideally, energy flows freely through them and in a balanced manner. When energy is not flowing freely, it leads to illness, emotional upset, etc.

The chakras are often referred to in tantric sex or yoga.

From bottom to top are the names of the chakras and where they are located.

1st : Root/Base : Base of the spine.

2nd: Sacral : Lower abdomen.

3rd : Solar Plexus : Upper abdomen.

4th : Heart : Just above the heart.

5th : Throat : Throat

6th : Third Eye : Forehead between the eyes.

7th : Crown : Very top of the head.

NAMASTE RITUAL

The Namaste ritual is a beautiful gesture of respect and love between you, your tantric partner, and the universe. Use it to begin and/or end your tantric meditations.

Kneel opposite one another. Rest your buttocks on your heels and put your hands together in the praying position.

Gaze into each other's eyes.

If it is the beginning of the meditation, raise your hands into the sky and bow to honor each other.

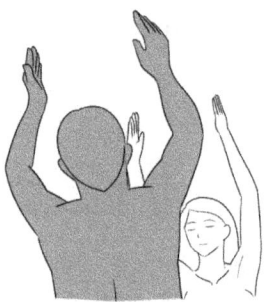

If you are closing the meditation with it, there is no need to raise your hands.

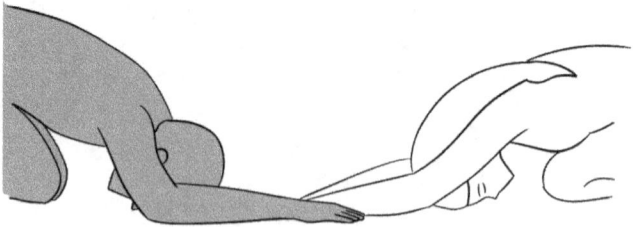

After the bow, bring your hands back into the prayer position, gaze into each other's eyes and say "Namaste" (na-mas-tay).

TANTRIC TASTE TEST

Sit naked across from your lover. Look deeply into their eyes, into their soul. Describe to each other how much you love and respect one another, and how you wish to become together in the universe.

Take each other's hands and close your eyes. Breathe deeply and in sync, inhaling and exhaling at the same time. Feel the energy flowing within yourselves and between your bodies, especially at your chakras.

Without touching each other, glide your hands around each other's bodies. Feel the warm energy radiating from each other.

Open your eyes and join hands again. Gaze into each other's souls. Continue to breathe in sync.

Concentrate on the energy flowing between you through your hands, breathing, and eyes.

When you're ready, slowly and softly touch each other's genitals. Once you are very wet and your partner is hard, or begin to make love.

When you are ready, or during sex, engage in the Yab Yum position.

Yab Yum

The Yab Yum position can be used to rest and/or embrace each other in a sexual or non-sexual way. It is a very intimate position, and is also good for being still and delaying orgasm. The man sits cross-legged, and the woman sits on top of him, wrapping her legs behind his back.

Related Chapters:

- Touch
- Chakras

BREATHING

Proper breathing plays a big part in connecting with yourself, your lover, and the universe. It is life force.

Full-Stomach Breathing

With your mouth closed, breathe in deeply through your nose. Count to four as you do so.

Your ribs and stomach expand as you fill up with air.

As you inhale, imagine your body and chakras being filled with the clear, positive energies of love and happiness.

When you cannot breathe in any more, hold the breath for a count of two, then fully exhale to a count of four through your nose and/or mouth, pushing your stomach to your spine.

Imagine all cloudy toxins, stress and negativity exiting your body.

Synchronized Breathing

Breathe in and out at the same time as your partner. This can be done at any time in any position, but is particularly good for sharing energy when spooning.

Circular Breathing

Sit opposite your partner and breathe deeply in sync, so that you are breathing in while they are breathing out.

As you breathe out and they breathe in, imagine the energy exiting your heart and entering theirs. As they breathe out and you breathe in, imagine the energy flowing out into the ground and back up into you. After a few minutes, swap it around.

This can also be done during sex.

Firing up Sexual Energy

As you inhale, use your hand to trace where it stops.

Lower your hand so each breath comes from your genitals.

Sitting Expansion

From a comfortable sitting position, compact yourself as much as possible.

Bring your elbows in and rest your hands on your head. Your spine will stretch.

As you inhale, expand your body.

Keep your hands where they are, but stretch your elbows as far back as you can and arch your back. Your chest will stretch.

Repeat.

Balloons

Allow your arms to dangle comfortably by your sides.

Exhale forcefully until your lungs are completely empty. Allow yourself to make noise.

Inhale just as forcefully, with as much or more sound. Continue this, being more forceful and louder with each breath.

Energizing Rapid Breath

With your arms outstretched to your sides, breathe rapidly through your nose. Pump your arms up and down. Your stomach should pulsate quickly.

Energizing Your Chakras

Sit back-to-back with your lover.

Direct your breath into your first chakra. Don't try to control it. Allow it to be chaotic and allow your body to move in the same fashion.

When you are ready, direct your breath into your second chakra in the same manner. Also allow your body to move. Continue in this way through all your chakras.

Once you reach the crown, work your way back down, allowing your breath to calm down. Once you are at your first chakra again, just feel your chakras vibrating in unison.

Note: Changing your position—sitting face to face or lying next to each other, for example—will change the sensations.

Lama Breaths

Stand with your feet shoulder-width apart and your knees slightly bent.

As you inhale, raise your arms to out to your sides. On the exhale, drop your arms to the side of your body. Allow sound to be expelled as you breathe out. Repeat this.

When you're ready, inhale and only raise one arm until you have a fist above your head. Drop it on the exhale, allowing sound to come out.

Alternate arms and repeat.

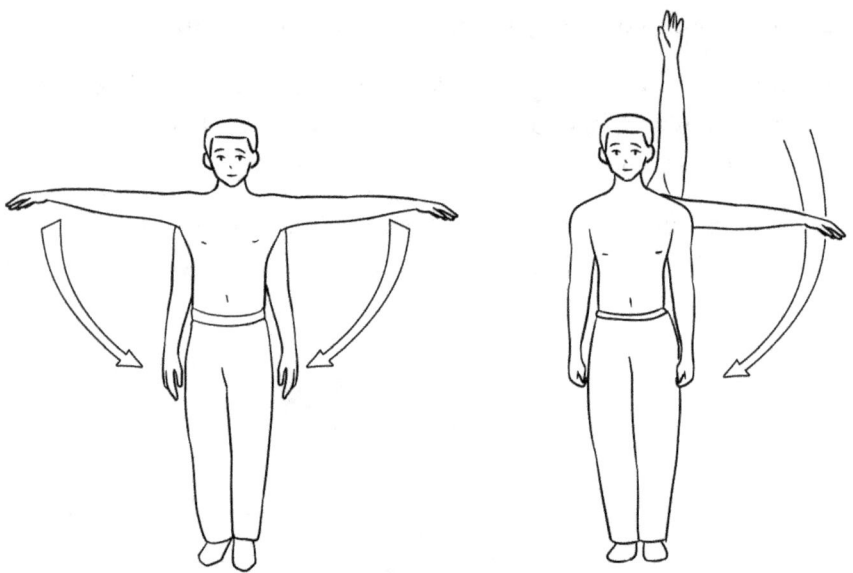

Related Chapters:

- Chakras
- Full-Stomach Breathing

UNDERSTANDING AND IMPROVING ORGASM

One of the keys to having amazing sex is to not focus on orgasm. In fact, focusing on orgasm often inhibits having amazing orgasms. Instead, enjoy your body for everything it is. Then when you do climax, it will feel incredible.

Note: Orgasms may release unexpected emotions. All reactions are healthy.

Her Orgasm

Women need mental focus much more and then men do to reach climax, and many women have never experienced orgasm. This may be due to low testosterone levels, but a more likely reason is psychological barriers.

Note: If it is due to low testosterone levels try switching to barrier methods of birth control (e.g., condoms) as other methods may be upsetting your hormonal balance.

The first step to overcoming psychological barriers is to feel good about orgasms and enjoy sex. It isn't a bad thing, it's amazing. If the barriers are deeply rooted—in sexual abuse, for instance—then a therapist may be helpful.

Going solo (masturbation) is the most reliable way for most women to experience their first orgasm. Go somewhere where you feel relaxed and won't be disturbed, and where you can express yourself freely. Don't try to control your body or worry about what it is doing. Just let it happen. Once you can give yourself an orgasm, it will be easier to have one with your lover.

Many women need more than just penetration to climax. Stimulate the clitoris at the same time.

Women: Never fake orgasms! It will only teach your lover how not to satisfy you.

Men: The only real way you can tell if a woman is having an orgasm is if you feel the intense contractions deep inside her vagina.

Simultaneous Orgasm

In order to climax together, you need to reach the same level of arousal at the same time. More often than not, it is the man who is ready to climax first. He can delay penetration until she is close, then with communication they can climax together.

Something to think about: If you climax together, you may be too focused on your own orgasm to fully experience the climax of your lover.

Multiple Orgasms

The key is to build up a greater level of sexual tension. Spend more time working each other up.

Men and women can have multiple orgasms. The only difference is that men will have a physical downtime that women will not. Men can achieve multiple orgasms without the downtime by strengthening their PC muscles. When you are close to ejaculation, tense your PC muscle to restrict the release of fluid while still feeling the contractions of the orgasm.

Note: Some consider this practice unnatural and dangerous.

After your first orgasm, the clitoris or penis may be too sensitive for more direct stimulation. Back off a bit. Shorten your down time by taking deep breaths and rocking your pelvis in time to your breathing.

Intensifying Orgasm

Stimulate erogenous zones during the orgasm and allow yourself to fully let go, making spontaneous and uncensored sounds and movement.If you have the fortitude, you can intensify your orgasm by foregoing it every two out of three times. Doing so increases desire and will intensify emotional and physical response in those times when you do allow yourself to orgasm.

Intensifying orgasm can also be achieved by strengthening your sexual muscles. Distinguishing between the two different muscles will become clearer as you strengthen them. Do these two exercises once a day, every day. Do 10-50 repetitions.

1. Sit or stand comfortably. As you breathe in, squeeze your anus, keeping the rest of your genital area relaxed. Breathe out and relax.
2. Breathe in deeply and hold your breath. Squeeze your genitals, making sure that the muscles in your anus are relaxed. Breathe out and relax.

PC (Pubococcygeal) Muscle

Strengthening the PC muscle is beneficial for everyone. Women can make their vaginas tighter and may also have stronger orgasms. Men have reported stronger erections and greater control of ejaculation. When you start and stop the flow of your urine, you are engaging your PC muscle.

Ways Women Can Exercise Their PC Muscle

- Tighten and relax the PC muscle 10 times in a row (10 reps). Do 10 sets of these, making a total of 100 reps. Do this twice a day, for 200 reps per day.
- Tighten and hold for three to seven seconds, and then release. Do 10 reps twice a day.

- Slowly tighten the PC muscle, stopping every now and again on the way up. Do 10 reps twice a day.
- When the PC muscle is strong enough, a woman can flex it during sex to grip her lover's penis. She may even be able to bring him to climax just by doing this.

Ways Men Can Exercise Their PC muscle

- Flex it 10 times in a row, for 10 sets per session, twice a day.
- A man can do it during intercourse to have his penis move inside his lover.

Tantric PC Exercise

Use your PC muscle to send your sexual energy through your body. As you engage the muscle, inhale through your nose. Hold your breath while you release and tense the muscle as many times as you can before you release your breath back out through your nose.

Tantric Orgasm

As you climax, tune into your body and surroundings, as opposed to blocking the world out by shutting your eyes. By doing so, you can achieve a state of bliss and your whole body will vibrate in orgasm.

As you approach climax, relax and let your body ease into it. Take deep, conscious breaths and focus on the feelings in every part of your body. As you climax, keep your eyes open and gaze into your lover's eyes.

Note: Although not necessary to achieve tantric orgasm, being in love will further enhance the experience.

After some practice, you can learn to store the sexual energy you and your lover create during sex in any part of your body, and then access it at will. You can also send the energy out into the universe through your crown chakra.

SELF-EXPLORATION

Explore your body. Learn what feels good to you. Start by giving yourself a full-bodied massage from head to toes. Take your time touching every part of your body. Use different pressures and strokes. Take deep breaths.

Erogenous Zones

Erogenous zones are the parts of the body that respond to sexual stimulation. Any part of the body may arouse a person, depending on the individual. Test by stroking, licking, sucking, kissing, caressing and gently biting any and all parts of your lover's body, taking note of what they respond to favorably.

Her Pleasure Points (Vagina)

Clitoris: As far as we know, the only purpose of the clitoris is to give women pleasure! It is located at the top of the labia, above the vagina, and is covered by the clitoral hood, which protects it from being constantly stimulated. This small bud-like erogenous zone swells with excitement, but once it is very aroused it may appear to disappear. Gentle rubbing usually feels fantastic to the owner.

G-spot: This area is about one third of the way up on the front wall of the vagina, and feels like a small swelling. When it is stimulated many women feel intense pleasure and some may even "ejaculate." Others may feel discomfort or numbness. Stimulate the G-spot by rubbing the making a "come here" motion with the pad of your finger, or use a vibrator with a special G-spot attachment.

Note: For double the pleasure, stimulate the clitoris and G-spot at the same time.

Perineum: The area of skin between the vagina and the anus. Use gentle strokes with your fingers or tongue.

His Pleasure Points (Penis)

Frenulum: The tiny bump of skin near the indentation on the underside of the penis.

Coronal ridge: The ring-like ridge around the head of the penis. Lick underneath it.

Perineum: The area of skin between the base of the penis and the anus. Use gentle strokes with your fingers or tongue.

Prostate gland: A small gland that lies below the bladder and can be stimulated via anal penetration. "Prostate" is not the same as prostrate.

Head: The smooth head of the penis.

Shaft: The area spanning from the base to the coronal ridge.

Scrotum: The sack that hangs below the penis and contains the testes.

Tantric Self-Exploration

Although these exercises are for self-exploration, they can also be done with a lover.

Emotional Release

Place something soft, which you can safely hit in front of you, such as some pillows. Have something from nature, like a leaf, next to you as well.

Put on some loud music; kneel before the pillows and release your anger into them. Bury your head in them, shout at them, and hit them. Become angry and use all the emotion you can. Shout anything you want.

Note: If you are doing this with your lover, you should not be able to hear each other's words.

When you feel like it, sit quietly. Express whatever emotions surface.

When everything is released and you are still, take your natural object and imagine all the clutter in your mind flowing into it, then return it to nature or give it to your lover to do so.

Friends with Nature

Go somewhere with nature around, such as a forest or a park. Walk around until a leaf (or flower, tree, etc.) "calls" you. Take the leaf and study it. Really feel it and see deep into it. Feel its life force.

Thought-Writing

Take a pen and paper and begin to write uncensored. Just write continuously, even if it doesn't make sense.

After five minutes, read the words out loud to yourself, being aware of how you are responding to what you read.

When you're ready, throw the paper away, along with all the clutter of your mind. Burn it if you wish.

Releasing Orgasmic Potential

Put on some loud, energetic music and get comfortable.

Begin to move your pelvis. Touch your genitals slowly and sensually. Massage your stomach, allowing your sexual energy to flow into it. Make any sounds you wish.

Continue to move however you feel, letting your hands roam anywhere on your body. Allow the energy to rise up through your solar plexus into and your heart. Allow the pressure to build until the energy finally bursts through.

Release any emotions as they come and surrender to the universe.

Related Chapters:

- Touch
- Massage

MASTURBATION

Just like sex, masturbation is only unhealthy if it interferes negatively with your life or if it causes severe physical pain or damage. It is the best way to discover what you enjoy sexually.

Use what you learn from masturbation to enhance your sex life by talking about it with your lover. Masturbating in front of each other is another great way to learn. It is also highly erotic.

Start with scented candles and a long bath. After the bath, give yourself a full body massage whilst concentrating on your breathing.

Finally, stimulate yourself sexually. Don't think about the orgasm. Just enjoy the touch.

When you're ready, bring yourself to climax.

Mutual Masturbation

When you're getting your lover off, enjoy it. If it turns you on, then they will get even more turned on. You can masturbate yourself at the same time, or they can give you a hand.

Once you find a stroke they like focus on the rhythm and pressure, and don't forget about the rest of their body. Their genitalia may become very sensitive immediately after climax, so ease off.

Tease

Caress the area around your partner's genitals sensually, without directly stimulating them. Come close then move away again. Get closer and closer and then gradually skim the erogenous zone. Take your time, until your partner is very aroused.

Only then should you move in for masturbation, but continue to move away every now and again. Two steps forward and one step back.

When your partner is on the verge of orgasm, keep a steady pace and keep doing what they like most. After they climax, ease off, unless told not to.

For Him

- Use a back-and-forth motion from the base to the head.
- Concentrate on the head of the penis. Use one hand just on the head, and one going up and down the shaft.
- Use one hand to press down on the base of the penis, while the other goes up and down the shaft.
- Play with the scrotum and testicles at the same time as the penis.
- Holding the penis with your left hand, place your right palm across the head. After every up-and-down with your left hand, rub your right hand lightly in a circle on the head.
- Have both hands on the penis, one at the top and one at the bottom. As your top hand comes down, bring your bottom hand up. Your hands should meet in the middle. Then, as your bottom hand goes back down, bring your top hand back up. Repeat.
- Use the same technique as above, but twist each hand a little as you do it.
- Use your thumb and forefinger to form a ring around the penis. Do it with both hands. Run your fingers up and down the penis any way you want: up and down together, with a twist, in opposite directions, etc.
- Coat your hands with a mild skin scrub. Gently roll the penis back and forward between your hands.
- Wrap a thin or silky scarf around the penis and use a gentle

stroke, twisting occasionally. Move the skin under the scarf or move the scarf itself.
- Fill a condom with as much jelly as it will hold (warm or cold) then put it on the penis. Expect jelly to displace. Once it has settled, hold the condom tight at the opening to seal the remaining jelly in. Use your other hand on the shaft.
- Grip the top of the penis with your left hand and place the right hand underneath the testicles, with your fingers pointing toward the anus. As you slide your left hand down, bring your right hand up, so they meet near the base of the penis. From here, slide your left hand back up the penis and your right hand back down, toward the anus.
- When ejaculation begins, clasp your two hands around the head of the penis. Squeeze gently and release in time with the contractions.
- Lightly brush your fingers up the shaft and around the tip.
- Work your hand up and down, tightening and releasing your grip as you go.
- Put the penis between your two open hands. Roll it in your palms as you move up and down.
- Gently toss the penis from one hand to another.
- Firmly hold the base with one hand. With your other hand, alternate between making circles at the tip and pulling the head up while gently twisting it.
- With your hands, squeeze the muscles that connect the thigh with the genital area.

For Her

- Lubrication, either natural or store-bought, is great for everyone, but a woman needs it to get a pleasurable experience more than a man does.
- Stimulate the clitoris by rubbing it directly or with a pillow, water flow from the shower, dildo, etc.

- Rub on or pull at the skin above and around the clitoris.
- Penetrate the vagina with your fingers or an object while also providing clitoral stimulation.
- When climaxing, place your hand over the pubic mound, with your fingers curved inside the front of the vagina, and pull up with slight pressure. You can pulse your fingers in time with the contractions.
- Many women report that the area to the left of their clitoris (as they look down), when rubbed, gives the most pleasure.
- Pull back the clitoral hood with one hand and stimulate the tip of the clitoris.
- Use a short up-and-down stroke on one side of the clitoris.
- Twirl your finger on the clitoral head, then around it. Move in both directions.
- Stimulate the lower part of the vaginal entrance, where it meets with the perineum.
- Push down on the G-spot with the pads of your finger(s) with varying pressures.
- Use your thumbs to twirl around the nipples, then at the far side of each breast.
- Stroke the perineum with two fingers while using your thumb on the clitoris.
- Rub the clitoral tip in circles, using a feather-light touch.
- If direct clitoral stimulation is too intense, rub on top of the clitoral hood.
- Rub around the vagina and labia.
- Rub up and down the opening between the labia, on the labia, and around the vagina.
- Stimulate the clitoris and the G-spot at the same time.

Tantric Hand Job

As you pleasure your lover in this way, compliment them throughout the whole process.

Your lover lies comfortably on their back. Run your hands smoothly over their body, and then let them rest, one at the top of the spine and one at the base of the spine. If either of these spots is cold, warm it up with your love energy.

Oil your lover's skin liberally and use your whole body to rub them all over. Rub their back and legs, then turn them over and rub their chest. Gaze into your lover's eyes and encourage sounds of pleasure.

Run your hands from the groin to the heart to transfer sexual energy into love. Send your love through your hands as well.

After you have massaged your lover's entire body, concentrate on their groin. If they are going to climax, just ease off for a while until their excitement subsides. You can continue to move energy from the groin to the heart.

Reassure them that climax or even arousal (including erections or wetness) is not important. Just feeling the pleasure of touch is amazing, and if arousal or climax happens then that is also fine.

Continue to rub the groin using any strokes you wish. Vary your touches and stay tuned into your lover's energy.

Related Chapters:

- Touch
- Massage
- Breathing

REDIRECTING SEXUAL ENERGY

When we are aroused, we build up a lot of energy. We can either release this energy or carry it round with us. We usually release it through climax. When you do not release it, you will experience what some may refer to as "sexual frustration," but in fact, if utilized in the right way, this energy can help people become very productive in their everyday lives.

We can make the most of this sexual energy by redirecting it throughout the body. By doing so, instead of feeling frustration when we are aroused but unable to release, we will feel energized throughout the body.

This redirection is also the first step in experiencing a full body orgasm, and as a more immediate result, is a great method of delaying climax in a man (or woman).

Redirecting Sexual Energy to Delay Climax

This can be adapted for other uses.

As soon as the man feels the point of no return, he uses breathing techniques as previously described, and he or his lover sweeps the energy from his groin to wherever he wants it. For example, they may:

- Gently massage the testicles then stroke down his thighs and up his belly to his heart.
- Draw the energy from the penis up through his spine into his heart.

To charge energy from her into him, his lover can sweep the energy from his penis to his heart, then into her heart and out of her vagina back into his penis.

Following the Snake

During other tantric exercises, you may build up so much energy that it courses up your spine.

Go with it and you can experience higher states of being.

Related Chapters:

- Breathing

PEAKING

Peaking is an exercise that can be done during intercourse or masturbation. It is an effective way for men to last longer. It can also be used by either sex to build up sexual energy, which will increase sexual pleasure. It is done by starting and stopping stimulation at various stages of arousal.

First find your point of no return. Give the stages of your arousal a scale from zero to 10. Zero is no arousal and ten is orgasm. Nine is your point of no return—that is, the point where it wouldn't matter if you stopped stimulation; you would still climax. You want to get to a 7 or 8 and stay there until you choose to climax.

Once you reach level 8, stop stimulation and re-direct your focus. Once your arousal has gone down to a 5 or 6, restart stimulation. Do this a few times before allowing yourself to climax. Other patterns you can use are:

- Peak, plateau, peak higher, plateau etc.
- Peak, plateau, decrease, peak a little higher than before, decrease, peak a little higher still, etc.

You can also try any other patterns you can think of until you discover what will work to control your arousal level without having to stop completely. Make a goal to last 30 minutes without stopping.

If needed, you can use peaking during intercourse by taking your penis out and changing positions, massaging, switching to oral stimulation, etc., until your arousal goes down.

Tantric Peaking

For this to work, the man must be adept at controlling his climax.

As you make love, allow the sexual energy to grow naturally. After about 20 minutes, you may feel a decrease in sexual energy. Allow this to happen and just relax in this state together. Stay inside your lover, even if your penis becomes soft. After a while, your sexual energy will return and you can attain a higher feeling of ecstasy. Move however you wish. Allow this increase and decrease of sexual energy to happen as many times as you wish. When you're ready, allow yourselves to climax.

Related Chapters:

- Masturbation

TANTRIC MASSAGE

Basic Tantric Massage

Your lover lies on their front. Massage their whole back and when ready, concentrate on the lower back. Guide the energy from here up the spine. Next, massage the head, back of the legs and feet. Take your time.

Your lover turns over. If he is a man, massage his belly with sweeping clockwise movements around his navel. If she is a woman, massage her lower abdomen in the same manner. Rest your hands on your lover's solar plexus and synchronize your breathing.

When ready, sweep up over their chest and shoulders and down their arms and hands, then continue to massage their arms and hands.

When you're ready, come back to massaging the chest, then sweep up the middle of their chest (between the breasts if they're a woman) and towards their throat.

Rest your hand on their heart, with your other hand between the eyebrows. Next, massage their neck and throat. Rest one hand on their throat and the other on the back of the neck. When ready, massage their head, face, and scalp.

Move down and massage their groin. If your lover is a man, pay special attention to his perineum then continue to massage his penis and testicles. If she is a woman, massage her pubic mound and around her vagina.

Finish with whole-body sweeps: down the legs, then back up over the chest and down the arms.

Tantric Chakra Massage

Your lover lies naked.

Oil up your fingers and apply the oil in a slow clockwise motion to the first chakra for a few minutes.

Rest your hand there for a moment to feel the energy expanding before reapplying oil and moving on to the second chakra. Continue this process up through all the chakras.

When you get to the sixth chakra, use gentle upward sweeps from in between your lover's eyebrows to their hairline.

Do not apply oil for the seventh chakra, and return to a clockwise rubbing.

When ready, place one hand on the first chakra and one on the seventh. Imagine the energy between the chakras connecting through your lover's body.

Related Chapters:

- Chakras

TANTRIC DANCING

Seductively Solo

Find somewhere private, where you will not be disturbed. Put on some music you will enjoy dancing to in a sexy manner.

Begin to dance as if your lover is watching you. Slowly and sensually remove your clothing for your lover. Imagine them being in awe of your beauty.

Once you are completely naked, dance uninhibited. Feel the sexual energy rising through your chakras. Caress yourself as you move.

When you are ready, lie down and continue to caress yourself.

Touch every inch of your body, imagining you are being touched by your lover. Bring yourself to orgasm if you wish.

Releasing Stress through Dance

You can release any stress held in your body with by dancing to your choice of music. Let your body move as it wants. Shake and make noise so everything comes out.

The Dance of Two Snakes

Dance back-to-back with your lover, but do not lean back into them.

Imagine a snake sitting at the base of your spine and working its way up. Let your body move with the snake as it climbs up your back.

As it reaches your arms, allow them to rise so the snake can uncoil further up and out of your hands.

Feel the serpent collecting energy from the universe above and feeding back down your body through your chakras. The energy and the snake should weave around each other, vibrating in your body.

When you're ready, face your lover and join at your foreheads, merging your energies.

The Calming of the Tribal Urge

Put on some "animalistic" or "tribal-ish" music to dance to.

Dance with your lover, undressing as you do so, until you're both naked. Build up your sexual energy as you move. Focus your energy into your genitals while you gaze into each other's souls. Feel the desire for sex rising. When you're ready, give in to your desires, but do not climax.

Allow the intensity to diminish and just lay together, with your lover still inside you, or vice versa.

When your/his erection is no more, stand and face each other.

Play some easygoing music and dance for each other once again.

When you're ready, lay down and embrace each other. Breathe circularly, then just lay still together.

Body Shake

Put on some music to make you move and begin to shake only your right leg. Next, shake your left leg, then your hips, arms, hands, shoulders, and your head. Keep adding body parts until your whole body is moving to the beat.

Related Chapters:

- Touch
- Chakras

TANTRIC ORAL

While giving mutual oral pleasure, you both imagine love energy flowing through your touch into your lover, thus building a circle of energy.

Whilst you are giving your partner exclusive oral pleasure, they vocalize whatever comes into the mind. It is uncensored and may or may not make sense.

Blindfold your lover and have them lie down. Taste their body all over and begin to give them oral pleasure. Indulge in your lover's taste. Allow the energy to flow between you. Do not bring your lover to climax. Instead, bring them close, then let the energy subside. Repeat the rising and subsiding of climax a number of times to build up energy.

When you are ready, place one hand on your lover's vagina or penis and the other on their heart or crown. Have your lover release the energy throughout their body.

Swap positions, and then bring each other to climax.

SEXUAL POSES FOR TANTRIC SEX

The best positions to use during tantric sex are those in which lovers feel most connected with your lover, and can look into each other's eyes and hold each other close.

Lotus

She crosses her ankles and draws her knees up. He kneels with his knees on either side of her and leans over her, resting on his hands. He can lean into her legs if she is flexible enough.

Clasping

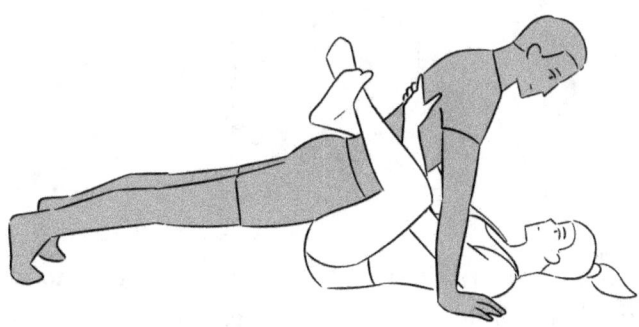

She lies on her back with her legs spread. He puts his groin to hers, keeping his body straight and supporting his weight on his toes and hands. She crosses her ankles around his waist. He presses his hips down, while pushing his upper body up off the floor at the same time.

Face to Face

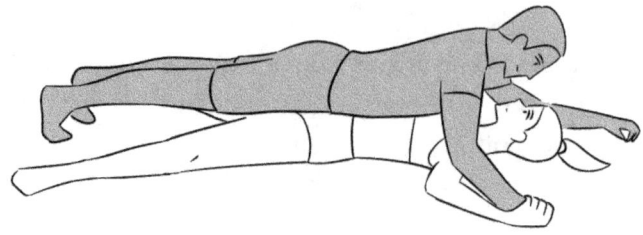

She lies flat on her back, legs spread. He lies on top of her, with his groin on hers. His legs are straight and his feet are together. He supports his weight on his toes. They grab each other's hands. He pushes down with his hips while lifting his upper body.

Yin and Yang

This is also known as Yab Yum. He sits cross-legged and she sits on top of him. They hold each other close, and she crosses her legs around his back.

AFTER CLIMAX

After either or both of you have climaxed, sit up in Yab Yum with your lover still inside you, or vice versa.

Take a deep breath in and picture drawing the energy of the ejaculation up the spine.

As you exhale, picture a golden mist coming down the spine.

30 MORE TANTRIC MEDITATIONS AND EXERCISES

Balancing Sexual Energy

Put your right index finger on the top of your nose between your eyes.

Exhale hard through your nose.

Close your right nostril with your thumb and breathe in to the count of seven. Release your right nostril and close your left nostril with your middle finger. Breathe out forcefully.

Continue to alternate the nostril you breathe in and out from. You can enhance the practice by contracting your PC muscle.

To stimulate your masculine energy, turn your head to the left and block your left nostril while you breathe. To stimulate your feminine energy, block your right nostril and turn your head to the right.

Bathing

While in the shower with your lover, soap up and turn your backs to each other. Rub against each other.

Cycling Love Energy

Place your right hand on your lover's heart while your lover does the same to you.

Visualize sending love energy from your heart down your arm and into your lover's heart.

Your left hand can be placed on any of yours or your lover's chakras in order to circulate the energy. Place it where ever you want the energy to go.

Divine Admiration

Slowly remove your lover's clothes.

As you expose each new part of their body, you both become aware of it.

When your lover is completely naked, they sit or lie down.

Caress each part of your lover's body, admiring it verbally as you go. For example, say, "These are the thighs of a magnificent being" or "These are beautiful buttocks," etc. When you've finished, transition to sex or just lie together.

Energy Focus

Sit back-to-back with your lover. Be close, but do not touch each other.

Close your eyes and focus on your spine. Shut off your attention to everything but the energy in between your two spines.

Energy Reading

Sit in the Yab Yum and synchronize your breathing.

When ready, close your eyes and let your hands explore your lover's body.

Whenever you feel like it, let your hands relax on a part of their body and say whatever comes into your mind, uncensored.

Food Play

Prepare a plate of bite-sized natural foods and include a glass of wine. Savor each bite and meditate on the flavors as if it is the first time you've tasted them. Being blindfolded will enhance the sense of taste.

Your lover is blindfolded and lies back comfortably while you feed them. Allow time for them to experience the smells, tastes, and textures of each piece, then pour a little wine into their mouth and allow them to experience it fully. Swap roles when you're ready.

Try these exercises in complete silence, and/or just enjoy a meal together outdoors without talking to each other.

Internal Listening

Put your thumbs in your ears and your fingers on the top of your head.

Listen to your breathing and any other internal sounds.

Laugh

Lie next to each other. Relax and stretch for a few minutes.

Laugh freely from your abdomens. Focus on your base chakras opening up. When your laughter naturally subsides, lie quietly and feel the sexual energy course through your bodies.

Lion Play

In a playful manner, both of you become lions.

Make sounds and move as lions would. When you are ready, approach each other.

Become territorial and ward each other off. Growl and circle warily. Become a little more aggressive and push on each other's paws, roaring loudly.

When you're ready and you naturally calm down, investigate each other. Smell and lick each other as wild beasts would. Become comfortable with each other. You may choose to mate, or just lie together as lions would. Afterward, come back to your human forms.

Moving Energy

Use your imagination and physical touch to move yours and/or your lover's energy around their body. You can move the energy to where ever you think it is needed.

While stimulating their genitals with one hand, imagine your breath going through your hand and into your lover's body. Use your other hand to move the energy to whichever chakra you want it to go to.

As you breathe back in, imagine the energy flowing back up from the chakra into your hand and cycling through your bodies. Keep breathing and visualizing the energy with your hands in these positions to create a cycle of energy. You can move the energy to other chakras if you wish.

Music

Play your favorite music. Lie comfortable with your eyes closed and listen intently, letting the music fill your body. This can also be done with nature. That is, you can lie/sit outside and just listen to the sounds of nature.

Om

Sit opposite each other and synchronize your breathing.

When you're ready, chant "Ommmmm" together. Feel the vibration in your bodies and let it build naturally.

Opening of the Chakras

Exhale and thrust your pelvis forward, saying "Ooooo." Inhale and bend your back forward, saying, "Aaahhhhh." Repeat.

Do the same exercise using "ooooo" on the exhale and "ehhhhhh" on the inhale, then using "oooo" and "uhhh."

Pelvic Thrusts

These can be done lying, squatting or standing. You can also change positions as you do them.

As you exhale, thrust your pelvis forward. On the inhale, thrust your pelvis backward. Swing your arms in time with your thrusts.

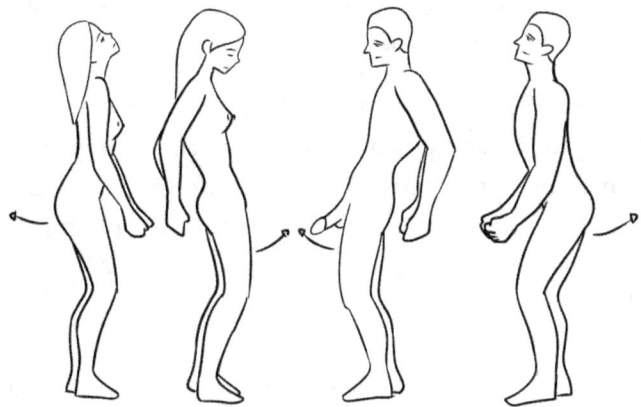

Praising Each Other

Sit together and think of three things you love or admire about your lover.

Take turns telling each other the three things, calling each other by name. For example, say "Mike, I really love the way you..."

Quenched Desires

Enter a meditative state.

You are the master and your lover is your servant. They will fulfill all your wishes.

Demand anything you want from them. Take as long as you need to fulfill all your desires. Next time, swap roles.

Returning to Earth

Stand opposite each other and visualize a spiral of energy from your heads to your groins.

Dance freely and make whatever sounds you want.

When you feel like it, calm down into cross-legged sitting positions, facing each other with your knees touching. Breathe in sync while swaying to loosen your bodies.

Breathe in and out of each of your chakras, starting from your base chakra. Move your way up your bodies until the energy is gathered at your crowns. Let this energy expand through your bodies and out into the universe. Lie down together for as long as you wish.

Sacrum Tap

Lay your lover on their stomach and tap on the area above their tailbone and below their waist. Next, run your thumbs up your lover's spine. Continue by tapping up on either side of your lover's spine with your fingertips. Finish with massage.

Seeing Your Lovers Soul

Sit opposite your lover and gaze into each other's eyes.

Begin full-stomach breathing and let all other concerns subside.

Do not speak. Look further into your lover's eyes. See their soul. Do this for as long as you wish.

Sensory Pleasure

Prepare a variety of pleasant scents and some fruits.

Blindfold your lover and get him/her to sit or lie down comfortably.

Introduce the different scents to your lover. They should smell each one deeply and separately. Next, take a piece of fruit and release its aroma by gently squeezing it.

Let your lover smell the fruit then place it on their lips so they know to allow you to place it in their mouth. Your lover should fully experience the taste and texture of the fruit, then allow the taste and smell to combine.

Swap roles.

Then, with both of you blindfolded, taste and smell each other in the same manner. Finish by making love, still blindfolded.

Sex Magic

Use visualization to manifest what you want from the universe.

Lie relaxed and visualize what you want.

Imagine sexual energy coursing through your body, enhancing the feeling you have when you have whatever it is you want.

When you are having sex or masturbating, recall this visualization and feeling, especially during high-pleasure states, including orgasm.

Sharing Desires

The two of you will share whatever desires come to your mind. They can be sexual or non-sexual.

Take turns saying "I want ..." and then say whatever comes to your mind.

Don't censor it. Everything is OK, including silence.

Sharing Loves Nature

Sit or kneel side by side with your lover. Get comfortable.

Each of you place a natural object of your choice, such as a flower or pebble, in front of you.

Take a couple of minutes to confide in your respective objects about your relationship.

Talk as if your lover was not there—that is, using the third person. Say anything you feel, positive or negative. This might be "I feel something is bothering her" or "I love the way he touches me when we make love," etc.

Continue to alternate who is talking every few minutes until the both of you feel you have finished sharing. Don't interrupt your lover when it is their turn.

Once you are finished, pick up your objects and imagine all the clutter in your minds flowing into them.

Place your object next to your lover, then place your head on the ground and ask for guidance from the universe. Drop all expectations and allow the wisdom to enter your mind, no matter what it is. If you wish, share the wisdom with your lover. Finish by taking your lover's object and returning it to nature, while they do the same for you.

Shiva Shakti Mudra

This is very effective for building energy.

Stand with your feet shoulder-width apart and with your knees slightly bent.

Take a few full-stomach breaths and get centered.

When you are ready, on the inhale sweep your arms up to collect the energy from the earth and bring it into your heart.

Exhale.

Inhale again, but this time, reach up to the sky and gather energy from the sky.

Sweep your arms down, crossing your hands over each other as you pass your face and pour the energy into your heart.

You can also send the energy out to others, like your lover or the world in general, by aiming your arms at them as opposed to into your heart.

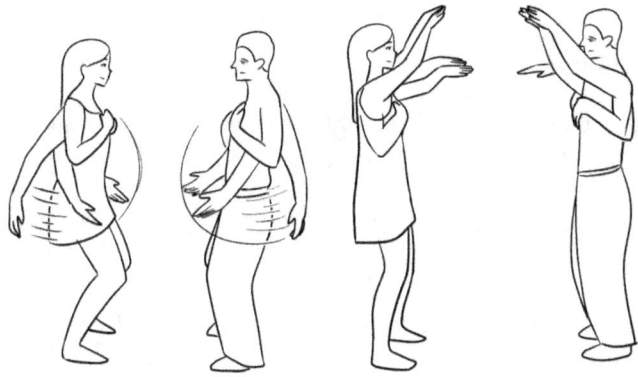

Singing

Blindfold your lover.

Hum a tune and whisper in their ear. Sing for your lover. Play an instrument if you wish.

Swap roles.

Smell

Take a shower together using only water or non-synthetic products so you do not overpower your natural scents.

Put on a blindfold and then smell all over your lover's body. Swap roles when you're ready. Finish with blindfolded sex.

Soulful Embrace

As you gaze into each other's eyes, slowly come together and embrace each other.

Synchronize your breath and become one.

When you're ready, separate slowly. Maintain eye contact as you separate.

Tantric Triangle

Visualize a triangle of white light in between your eyes, pointing down toward the back of your tongue.

Taste

Lightly touch around your lover's mouth and lips. Begin to touch the rest of their face.

Blindfold your lover and feed them various bite-sized foods of different tastes and textures.

Related Chapters:

- Food Play
- Touch
- Massage
- Chakras
- Full-Stomach Breathing
- Breathing

THANKS FOR READING

Dear reader,

Thank you for reading *How to Have Great Sex*.

If you enjoyed this book, please leave a review where you bought it. It helps more than most people think.

Don't forget your FREE book chapters!

You will also be among the first to know of FREE review copies, discount offers, bonus content, and more.

Go to:

https://offers.SFNonfictionBooks.com/Free-Chapters

Thanks again for your support.

REFERENCES

Gray, J. (2012). *Men Are from Mars, Women Are from Venus.* Harper-Element.

Greaux, J. Langheld J. (2007). *Better Sex Through Yoga: Easy Routines to Boost Your Sex Drive, Enhance Physical Pleasure, and Spice Up Your Bedroom Life.* Harmony.

Jameson, J. Strauss, N. (2012). *How to Make Love Like a Porn Star: A Cautionary Tale.* It Books.

Lalvani, V. (2002). *Yoga for Sex: Improve Your Sex Life the Tantric Way.* Bounty Books.

Nerve.com. (2003). *Position of the Day: Sex Every Day in Every Way.* Chronicle Books.

Richardson, D. (2003). *The Heart of Tantric Sex: A Unique Guide to Love and Sexual Fulfillment.* Bedroom Books.

Richardson, D. Richardson, M. (2010). *Tantric Sex for Men: Making Love a Meditation.* Destiny Books.

Riley, D. Riley, K. (2002). *Tantric Secrets for Men: What Every Woman Will Want Her Man to Know about Enhancing Sexual Ecstasy.* Destiny Books.

Strauss, N. (2009). *Rules of the Game.* It Books.

Vatsyayana. (2012). *The Kamasutra.* YogaVidya.com.

AUTHOR RECOMMENDATIONS

Discover How to Use Yoga as Medicine

Add this book to your collection, because with it you can use yoga to heal your mind, body, and spirit.

Get it now.

www.SFNonfictionBooks.com/Curing-Yoga

Teach Yourself to Meditate

Discover your inner peace, because this book has 160+ meditations to choose from.

Get it now.

www.SFNonfictionBooks.com/Meditation-Workbook

ABOUT AVENTURAS

Aventuras has three passions: travel, writing, and self-improvement. She is also blessed (or cursed) with an insatiable thirst for general knowledge.

Combining these things, Miss Viaje spends her time exploring the world and learning. She takes what she discovers and shares it through her books.

www.SFNonfictionBooks.com

amazon.com/author/aventuras
goodreads.com/AventurasDeViaje
facebook.com/AuthorAventuras
instagram.com/AuthorAventuras

www.ingramcontent.com/pod-product-compliance
Lightning Source LLC
Chambersburg PA
CBHW071219080526
44587CB00013BA/1431